UNLOCK THE HIDDEN POWER OF YOUR MIND!

In these pages you will discover the method to help you achieve your inner dream—whether it is attaining material riches or spiritual gifts.

* You will learn how to tap the psychic memory bank of the universe and discover secrets that can make you healthy, happy and successful.

* You will learn how to have prophetic and clairvoyant visions which will show you how to avoid danger and know your future.

* You will be shown how to tune in on the constructive thoughts of other people and use them creatively in your own life.

* You will see how you can solve your problems through the gift of psychic mediumship.

* You will discover the secret of precognition and how to know the future for yourself and others.

And much, much more!

HOW TO DEVELOP YOUR PSYCHIC POWERS FOR HEALTH, WEALTH, AND SECURITY

By Anthony Norvell

PAPERBACK LIBRARY

New York

PAPERBACK LIBRARY EDITION

First Printing: December, 1970

Library of Congress Catalog Card Number: 69-11731

This Paperback Library Edition is published by arrangement with
Parker Publishing Company, Inc.

Paperback Library is a division of Coronet Communications, Inc.
Its trademark, consisting of the words "Paperback Library"
accompanied by an open book, is registered in the United States
Patent Office. *Coronet Communications, Inc., 315 Park Avenue
South, New York, N.Y. 10010.*

I dedicate this book to my many students who studied and worked with me in my investigation of the entire field of Parapsychology during the years I lectured at Carnegie Hall. I wish to express to all these students my appreciation for permitting me to use some of their experiences in the field of Psychic Phenomena as illustrations in this book.

What This Book Can Do for You

You can tap amazing psychic forces that exist in the universe and channel them to every department of your life for health, wealth, happiness, daily and future security.

You can project psychic thought forms to other minds and imprint them with your ideas and suggestions. You have the ability to probe the cosmic memory bank of the universe and discover secrets which geniuses of the past used to create great works.

The universe is filled with a flood-tide of psychic intelligence which permeates every atom and cell of earth and space. This psychic guidance extends to all living creatures and shows them how to evolve to their right destiny.

The caterpillar knows how to tap Cosmic Mind and learn how to weave a cocoon and become a butterfly.

The homing pigeon instinctively knows how to fly hundreds of miles back to its starting place, without a compass.

The bee creates a six-sided honeycomb knowing by some psychic means that it will store more honey than a four or five-sided comb.

The spider weaves a perfect geometric web without any prior mathematical instruction.

We see evidence of this Cosmic and Psychic Intelligence between the planets and the earth. The moon radiates its Cosmic message from two hundred and fifty thousand miles away with a command to the earth's billions of tons of water and is able to cause the tides to ebb and flow.

The acorn knows by some instinctive knowledge how to break out of its prison house, take root and become a hundred foot oak tree.

The chick within its egg is given some kind of cosmic and psychic prompting, which tells it how to create feathers, a beak, heart, kidneys, lungs, eyes and ears. Then it is told by the cosmic memory bank of the universe to break out of its shell in twenty-one days.

But these cosmic and psychic miracles in the realm of nature are as nothing compared to the miraculous creation of a human being. Here it is that a complete telepathic system of communication is set up between the Cosmic Mind and the mother's body, which can, in nine month's time create the miracle of a living, breathing, thinking, sensing being that evolves and matures according to a cosmic and biological time clock that has been set since the beginning of time.

Think of the psychic promptings that go out from the human consciousness, telling the pituitary gland when to stop secreting its growth hormone so the body will stop growing.

Consider the mystery of psychic communication which occurs in the bones of a growing child. The little messengers, created in the marrow for that function, run to the outside of the joints to deposit calcium until the bones grow to their normal length, then some psychic command tells them their work is finished and they quietly die and disappear.

Truly, man lives in a world of psychic wonders! Surrounded on all sides by invisible cosmic forces he may become so psychically attuned to this higher Cosmic Mind that he can literally perform miracles in his life.

PSYCHIC GUIDANCE CAN BRING YOU ACHIEVEMENT OF EVERYTHING YOU DESIRE

Just as everything in nature operates under this dynamic, psychic principle, so too, your higher psychic centers can be trained to receive cosmic pulsations that will guide you to the achievement of everything you desire in your life.

You can use this higher psychic power to give you health and keep you vibrantly healthy and strong for a hundred years or more.

You can be guided through psychic vision to safety in your life and achieve security and fulfillment of your life's dream.

You can tap the strata of universal magnetism through psychic vision and attract to yourself money, fame, power, people—and utilize them for your future growth and fulfillment.

You can tap this psychic stream of Cosmic Intelligence and *Know the Future,* as surely as that crawling caterpillar knows it is to become a butterfly.

You can use psychic vision to show you how to make a million dollars, if you choose. You can be shown how to invest your money and build a great financial empire.

You can use mental telepathy to communicate with those who are in distant places and receive their psychic messages as easily as you now telephone a friend across the continent.

You can develop powers of clairvoyance, ability to see with the inner eye—clairaudience, ability to hear with an inner ear, the things that exist in an invisible, fourth-dimensional world where matter is no barrier to Cosmic Mind. You can know the past, and through the psychic gift of precognition, you can know the future as definitely as the maple tree knows in winter that its sap is to be stored in its roots. But when spring arrives, some psychic prompting causes that tree to send the sap up into its trunk and branches, and adorn the tree with leaves.

You can learn how to use psychic somnambulism to achieve astral projection while you sleep. Your soul can go out into time and space and explore the mysteries of the universe and visit distant places in past history or project itself to the future dimensions of time and space.

Extrasensory perception and psychic phenomena have been proved a reality by our modern scientists. They now know that some great Cosmic Intelligence ties the universe together with invisible lines of psychic communication. They know that the soul is a reality; that it has mystical powers for knowing secrets of the universe and that man is guided by a higher intelligence than his own conscious mind.

Let us now study together the methods by which you can build your own psychic powers. Only one attribute is needed: have faith in this Cosmic-psychic intelligence and know that it exists and that it may be channeled for your greater good.

ANTHONY NORVELL

Twenty-Five Reasons Why This Book Will Help You

1. You will learn how to tap the psychic memory bank of the universe and discover secrets that can make you healthy, happy and successful.

2. You will learn how to have prophetic and clairvoyant vision which will show you how to avoid danger and know your future.

3. You will be shown how to tune in on the constructive thoughts of other people and use them creatively in your own life.

4. You can solve your problems through the gift of psychic mediumship.

5. You will tap the higher intuitive Mind which will guide you each day in building your life on safe, secure principles.

6. You will learn about psychic projection of thought forms and ideas, which will enable you to reach others in distant places.

7. Through telepathic communication you will be able to receive thoughts from other minds which may warn you of their actions so you can protect yourself against unscrupulous persons.

8. You can channel any gifts you choose from the Cosmic Mind and become a writer, inventor, composer, artist or businessman.

9. You will be shown how to have the all-knowing, all-seeing, all-powerful mind which comes from tapping the thoughts of great geniuses of the past.

10. You will be shown how to tap the fountain of youth and have vibrant energy and tremendous reserves of power so you can have a healthier body and live longer.

11. You will learn how to receive the psychic pulsations of the cosmos through your higher imagination.

12. You will learn how to use omniscience, omnipotence and omnipresence to show you how to discover lost articles and hidden treasures.

13. You will discover the secret of precognition and how to know the future for yourself and others.

14. You will discover the mirrorscope of the mind and soul, which will reflect the great thoughts from geniuses of the past.

15. You will discover the cosmic life energy and learn how to channel it into your mind and body for greater magnetism.

16. You will be shown how to put into the psychic portfolio the events you want in your future life, the money you desire, the experiences you wish to have and they will materialize for you.

17. You will be shown how to use your mind like a camera and projector to imprint everything you desire upon your psychic centers and then project them to the world of reality to make them come true.

18. You will be initiated into the mysteries of cosmic improvisations and learn the secret power that can make you as rich and famous as you want to be.

19. You will find out about psychic somnambulism and how you may take Astral journeys into the past or future.

20. You will find out about the psychic antenna of your higher mind and how to tune in on inspirational thoughts that are in the atmosphere or how to read the minds of others.

21. You will learn about the spiritual prototype which you can use to demonstrate unlimited power, money, health, success, love and friendship.

22. You can successfully use psychic mediumship to solve your every problem and be guided to a happy life.

23. You will be shown how to create the psychic matrix in your consciousness where all material things will be formed that you want to materialize in your outer life.

24. You can tune in on cosmic wavelengths as you tune in on radio and television, when you want to receive psychic guidance that warns you of danger and brings you security.

25. You will discover the universal secret of cosmic and psychic programming which will cause you to feed into the computer of your higher psychic mind every detail of the future life you wish to live.

Contents

ers. Example of penetrating emotion. A psychic projection of a home. Other types of psychic projection. Secrets of telepathic hypnosis. The four steps to take for telepathic hypnosis. How hypnotic telepathy healed marital infidelity. How you may receive psychic telepathy from others. The rules for psychic reception. How this psychic power worked a family reconciliation. Telepathic reception for investment information. How doubting a clairvoyant dream cost Peter big winnings.

How to make contact through psychic mind centers. How to achieve true serenity and power. How to become a creative genius. How to find lost articles. How psychic guidance led a person to a gold mine! How to build your faith in the cosmic mind power. How cosmic knowledge works in nature. The cosmic intelligence of you. The steps you may take to contact the fabulous psychic storehouse of cosmic memory. How a psychic dream led to finding a hidden fortune. How psychic projection worked a financial windfall. A dream of an event of danger. You possess a psychic time clock within you.

You may already be more psychic than you thought possible. Where psychic precognition is found. How psychic warnings came to these famous men. An instance of psychic precognition that could have protected a person. How psychic precognition saved a girl from death. The art of psychic castle-building. How to use psychic castle-building. The psychic kaleidoscope of inner soul power. Eight steps to take for using psychic precognition to mold and develop your future. How an inventor used psychic precognition to become wealthy. How a woman attracted a $5,000 mink coat for herself. How a woman selected her husband psychically.

*How a woman took astral flight to Italy. The time
barrier does not exist in the universe. How a doctor
averted tragedy through astral vision. Scientists
prove the existence of man's soul. Astral projection through a dream proved accurate. Soul's
remembrances often come masked as dreams. A
program for using psychic somnambulism to induce astral projection. Astral flight to the Bahamas
made this woman rich! Automatic writing or painting through the astral forces. How a business contact came through astral projection.*

*The tremendous reserves of psychic energy within
you. Most geniuses possessed this type of psychic
energy. How you can release psychic reserves of
energy through positive commands. The six forms
of psychic will you may unlock. How to invoke the
psychic will to live and be healthy. How to invoke
the psychic will to happiness and peace of mind.
How to invoke the psychic will to riches and success. How a widow secured psychic guidance. How
to invoke the psychic will to life fulfillment and
marriage. How a woman given up by doctors recovered. How to invoke the psychic will for creative gifts and talents. How this psychic power
gives you the answers. How psychic will changed a
woman's life. How to invoke the psychic will to
find security and permanency. This too shall pass
away.*

*Many persons use psychic mediumship to solve
problems. How to use psychic stimulators. Prob-
lem No. 1—Lack of money, poverty and related
problems. An insurance salesman's experience.
Problem No. 2—Relating to illness and accident.
A healing of a mysterious allergy. Problem No. 3
—Relating to business matters and relationships.
A healing of job unemployment. Problem No. 4—*

The overcoming of personality disorders, self-consciousness, inferiority and inadequacy. Problem No. 5—Overcoming negative habits, smoking, drinking, procrastination, laziness, gambling and excessive spending. Problem No. 6—Friction and discord in the home and work. How marital friction was solved. Problem No. 7—Overcoming general unhappiness, moodiness, depression and anxiety states. Problem No. 8—Relating to love and marriage failure. How to use psychic stimulators to help you. How a woman had psychic guidance in her marriage. Problem No. 9—Social problems, lack of popularity, lack of magnetism, loneliness and other related problems. How a young lady came alive socially.

How to make a psychic portfolio. Psychic guidance reveals the path. A program to increase your level of psychic awareness. How a woman's desire for her son materialized. How to find lost objects through this power. How valuable lost articles were found. How a woman found hidden treasures in Arizona. Questions to increase your level of psychic awareness. My psychic blueprint for future fulfillment.

How laws of psychic phenomena work in nature. A clairvoyant vision her sister would have twins. A psychic warning that a brother had died. Use these 10 dynamic laws to develop psychic powers, intuition and clairvoyance. Law No. 1—Invoke the law of self-preservation to unlock psychic powers. How a warning of danger came through psychic dream. Law No. 2—Express your psychic urge to evolve your creative ego to a higher level of activity. A woman ignored psychic warning and was sued. Law No. 3—Stimulate psychic vision through your imagination. Law No. 4—Release psychic energy through your emotions and by the power of concentration. Create and project psychic images through cosmography. How a woman educated her children through clairvoyant guidance. Law No. 5—Create spiritual magnetism to link you with the cosmic clearing house of all psychic communication. How money was magnetized through psychic projection. Law No. 6—Elevate your consciousness from the third-dimensional world of matter to the fourth-dimensional world of thought and spirit. Law No. 7—Use the law of psychic fusion of your soul with the soul of the universe. Psychic power is the universal language of the soul. Law No. 8—The dynamics of psychokinesis. How a baby's life was saved through psycho-dynamics. Psychic energy can move physical objects. Law No. 9—Use psychic replay to review the past and to project future events through the process of precognition and retrocognition. How to replay past events through retro-cognition. Law No. 10—Elevation of your consciousness to the cosmo-psychic realm.

How psychic short-circuiting stunted children's normal growth. How psychic centers control your body's functions. How short-circuiting occurs in the brain and body. The negative emotions that destroy cosmic magnetism. How negative emotions create death-dealing chemicals. Chemical poisoning produced monsters. The positive emotions which produce life-giving cosmic magnetism for health and long life. How to use positive emotions to build cosmic magnetism and health. Why people can live to be over one hundred. Follow your own psychic guidance in matters of health and long life.

Your mind as a sending and receiving station. How cosmic telepathy works in all nature. A telepathic system exists within your body cells. A psycho-cosmic body possesses the same power of psychic and cosmic telepathy. How I met the Duke and Duchess of Windsor through psychic projection. Regime for using psychic and cosmic telepathy to influence and attract important people. How a jewelry salesman sold with psychic projection. How an electrical gadget was sold. How I projected a meeting with William Randolph Hearst.

How psychic power gives man wings of the soul. Your soul's remembrance of the past. Invisible phantom thought forms are all around you. How to receive guidance from geniuses of the past through psychic attunement. How one writer tuned in on Thomas Wolfe. How an attorney wins court cases through this principle. An artist draws on the inspiration of Turner.

How psychic dynamics can give you new values

in life. The meaning of psychic dynamics. Unlocking the mystic doors of reality through psychic dynamics. How to use desire as a psychic dynamic key. How to use imagination as a psychic dynamic key. How to transform your negative environment with psychic dynamics. How you can use concentration as a psychic dynamic key to your future. Concentration stimulates the psycho-neural centers. How to use inspiration as a psychic dynamic key to give you security. Forces that release inspiration through psychic dynamics. How to use faith as a key of psychic dynamics.

How you can use the power of psycho-kinematics. How to use the power of psycho-kinematics to change your life for the better. How a girl projected the image of love and marriage. How a maid and butler attracted a fortune. How a woman projected a trip to Europe free. How this power worked in a social situation. How a great singer uses this secret to hold her audiences.

The three minds which man may use. How to use your conscious mind in psychic programming. How to use your subconscious mind in psychic programming. How to use your superconscious mind in psychic programming. How to use psychic stimulators for life-programming. Use these twenty-five psychic stimulators from great minds to set up chain reactions in the computer of your higher mind. How to feed psychic stimulators into your superconscious mind. Examples of successful psychic programming. How to use psychic sensors in your programming of future events. The ten positive forces to feed your psychic computer to overcome negative forces.

chapter 1

How to Have
Dynamic Health Through
Psychic Guidance

You possess the power to keep your body healthy, vital and young for a hundred years or more.

This dynamic power resides within the psychic centers of your brain—it is the intelligence within your cells which tells you what to eat; it digests your food and distributes the chemical elements throughout your body, nourishing, healing, repairing and energizing all your body organs.

This psychic power is the life force which began to stir in the centers of your brain with the very first breath you drew when you were born. It can continue guiding you to good health all your life; it is the power that keeps you breathing even at night, when you are sleeping; it makes your heart beat; it heals your body, repairs the damaged cells and causes the blood to flow to every part of your brain and body.

A PSYCHIC VOICE SPEAKS
TO YOUR BODY CELLS

You can learn how to listen to this higher psychic voice that speaks to your brain and body cells; you can follow its guidance every moment of your life. It will show you how to avoid sickness, how to kill invading bacteria, how to insulate yourself against sickness through the chemistry of your glands. It can release a perpetual flow of cosmic power that will keep your heart beating in dynamic rhythm to the pulsating heartbeat of the universe.

This higher psychic power, transmitted by your mother's mind, is the miraculous power that built your body perfectly in only nine months' time. It created blood, bone and tissue—billions of cells that formed your heart, brain, lungs, stomach, kidneys, nerves, arteries and bones. This psychic pattern for developing the unborn child is in the higher centers of the mother's consciousness and works under universal laws which can be understood and controlled.

It is this type of psychic power which gives you the ability to have dynamic health and long life.

MAN IS SURROUNDED BY PSYCHIC FORCES

Man lives in a world of mystery, surrounded on all sides by dynamic forces which he does not fully comprehend. He has his life and being in an invisible psychic realm which controls his every move and function in life.

Flowing throughout the cells of the entire universe there is a great psychic intelligence which obeys the promptings of a higher, Cosmic Mind. This intelligence manifests itself in nature through the invisible forces of gravity, magnetism, electricity, radioactive rays and capillary attraction in the soil.

It is in this realm of the fourth dimensional world that the laws of psychic phenomena operate in invisible wavelengths.

Your mind may tap this higher psychic power and channelize it to any department of your life, giving you better health, longer life, peace of mind, happiness, security, and love-fulfillment.

YOUR DESTINY SHOULD BE GREAT

This psychic intelligence is the invisible navigator at the helm of the ship of destiny, upon which we sail on a mystical journey through time and space. We are bound for mystic horizons of the mind and soul, beyond the barriers and limitations of physical matter. We are voyagers upon a glittering star, which man calls earth, spinning around the sun at one thousand miles per hour. We are

22

bound for a divine destiny, which can be transcendentally beautiful; we can have perfect health of mind and body; we can achieve high goals, if we obey the directions of this higher psychic mind.

Why is it, if man was created to know health, happiness and prosperity, that we are so often sick and miserable?

It is because we fail to listen to the psychic voice of guidance within. We ignore the divine promptings of intuition which can tell us how to live, how to be healthy, how to heal the body, if we should become sick.

HOW PSYCHIC POWER WORKS IN NATURE

This miraculous psychic intelligence works in the realm of nature, creating seeming miracles. All birds, animals and insects, as well as plants and trees, obey this higher intelligence without question. Guided by divine instinct, they fulfill their destinies perfectly. You do not see a horse or cow eating poisonous foods, drinking alcohol or smoking injurious cigarettes.

See how perfectly this psychic intelligence works within a chicken's fertilized egg. It appears to be a lifeless, un-intelligent form of matter, and yet, in its invisible, pro-tected center, there is a vital psychic life force which obeys the laws of a higher, Cosmic Intelligence. Within twenty-one days that dead, inert matter within the egg changes into pulsating life and produces feathers, heart, lungs, eyes that see, ears that hear, and a vital life force which causes the chick to peck its way out of the egg and fulfill its life destiny.

HOW TO RELEASE THE PSYCHIC LIFE FORCE

The intelligence of God's infinite mind, working through the laws of nature, can speak to your body cells and re-lease the psychic life force which can keep your body healthy. These divine promptings come to man through intuition and may be tapped by anyone who learns the language of the soul—which is psychic phenomena. This reserve life force within the cells can be fanned into vibrant life even when a person is sick and on the verge of death.

A doctor's psychic experience

A doctor once told me of a patient who was dying of several complications. He had been in a coma for three days and there seemed to be no way to arouse him. This doctor had known many psychic experiences and believed in a higher dimension of mind and soul. He decided to try an experiment. He talked to the unconscious man in a soft, gentle voice. He said, "You cannot die now. Your ten-year-old son would be left without a father. He will not be able to have a college education. His life will be difficult. You must live, you must get well, for your son's sake. You will hear my voice; you will come out of your coma and become completely healed and live. The life force within your brain and body will respond to my suggestions and you will awaken and be healthy once again."

Within two hours' time this patient came out of his coma; he ate a big meal and in a few days' time was out of bed and walking about. His symptoms seemed to have completely disappeared, and he returned to his work and had tremendous vitality and energy.

THE FIVE FUNCTIONS
OF PSYCHIC MECHANISM FOR HEALTH

There are five main functions of this higher psychic mechanism within your brain and body. By knowing these, you can learn how to release the miracle power of the subconscious mind and psychic radiation and keep your body functioning perfectly at all times.

1. To kill invading bacteria that might endanger life and to maintain perfect bodily health.

2. To heal the body if it should become sick or be injured by accident.

3. To operate the automatic functions of heart, lungs, bloodstream and digestion.

4. To nourish the body and distribute the various elements the body needs for perfect health.

5. To release the genetic mechanism in reproduction that transmits the various invisible elements within the life germ, to create new life and nourish it within the mother's womb.

HOW THIS PSYCHIC FORCE WORKS FOR HEALTH

This psychic mechanism within your higher mind keeps your body healthy by channelizing the magnetic and electrical currents that are in the great cosmic spaces of the universe. Science knows that our life force comes to us from the radioactive rays that bombard our earth from outer space. But there are other, more subtle radiations which your higher mind utilizes for maintaining perfect health. No one knows how the body breaks down the food we eat into its essential elements so the blood stream can take it to the billions of cells which need nourishment. This higher, psychic intelligence within the brain and body is the invisible intermediary which performs this highly complex and mysterious task without any outside guidance or help.

When you worry about vitamins, minerals and other elements, remember your grandparents and great-grandparents knew nothing about such things, and many of them lived to be very old. Their higher psychic brain centers caused them to eat what they required for bodily health and nourishment.

LOVE ———— THE PSYCHIC POWER THAT KEEPS ONE HEALTHY

It was found in a study of children from poor homes and rich homes, where the poor child had love and felt secure, even though his diet was inadequate, that his body remained perfectly nourished. The psychic ingredient of

LOVE made the difference in the chemical balance of his body. The rich children, from homes where there was an adequate, nourishing diet, but whose parents were divorced or where they lacked love and feelings of security, were undernourished, even though they received the best of foods. The vital element of psychic sufficiency, LOVE, was missing from their lives and their bodies were malnourished.

HOW HELPING OTHERS
HEALED AN ELDERLY WOMAN OF DIABETES

Very often the body will be given an impetus to new life and energy, which can heal it, when we are inspired to help others in life. Those who feel old, unwanted and unloved, often blossom under the impulse to help others live a better life and often become healed.

One member of our lecture group in New York was very sick with sugar diabetes and a number of other ailments. She was seventy-six when she came into our work, and the doctors had told her she could not expect to live much more than six months. When she learned about the psychic and cosmic forces which control all of life, she began to forget her symptoms of sickness; she busied herself with charity work, for her family did not need her, as they were all grown up and on their own. She listened to the psychic voice within, and it told her to become useful doing something good for humanity instead of sitting around thinking she was old and finished, and looking for new symptoms.

This lady applied to a children's hospital as a volunteer, and gave several hours a week to caring for motherless children. As she busied herself doing this creative work, the surge of life energy returned to her brain and body, and she told me a few weeks later that all her symptoms had disappeared. She became a dynamo of creative action. One day, while sitting in psychic reverie an idea came to her for a child's book of fantasy; she sat down and it came through her higher psychic centers automatically. She finished it and then asked for psychic guidance to a publisher. She was led to the source that immediately took her book and published it. She wrote another, and kept at her work with children, until finally she was so healthy and strong that she stopped taking daily shots of insulin and appeared normal and healthy in every respect. Her doctors said the change that had come over this lady was a miracle. Today she is still active and healthy, and has now begun doing water color illustrations for her children's books.

THE PSYCHIC REGIME
FOR VIBRANT GOOD HEALTH

1. *Put your conscious mind in tune with the higher psychic mind that controls your body.*

This is done through giving the subconscious mind, where this automatic power resides, POSITIVE SUGGESTIONS, that it can incorporate in the psychic pulsations that radiate to the body cells.

Every morning when you get up give these suggestions to this higher mind. The psychic centers of your brain will automatically transmit these suggestions through the nerves and muscles of your body, and create the conditions that you suggest. This is what scientists call *conditioned reflexes*. Remember—it is perfectly natural for your psychic response centers to maintain health and balance within your body cells; what you are doing in this positive approach is merely to implement that power by directing the psychic energy and life force within your brain and body cells into channels of health, vitality and youth.

Repeat each of these psychic suggestions over at least five times upon arising in the morning.

I am healthy, vital, strong and radiate dynamic energy.

The psychic centers of my higher mind are now attuned to the dynamic life currents in the invisible, and I channelize that power and energy from the Cosmos to every living cell of my brain and body.

I now attune my mind to the psychic image of

27

health and energy and my body responds with the release of chemicals that are essential to my body's health and strength.

I am infused with the psychic life force that animates all living things. I live in the conscious awareness of my power for life, energy and growth.

I direct the life force within me to maintain balance in all my chemical forces and to set up barriers against invading bacteria that might injure my health.

I am young and vital and every cell of my brain and body responds to the universal life force which constantly regenerates all living cells and animates them with pulsating life and energy.

2. *Implement the psychic force within your body through the positive element of faith.*

The emotions that you indulge have a great deal to do with the generating of psychic life energy within your brain and body. The emotion of faith is credited with more miracles than any other single emotion. Implement daily your faith in God, believe in the ability of your higher mind to channelize God's life forces within your body for maintaining perfect health.

Faith, coupled with prayer, is truly a psychic miracle worker.

3. *Use the positive forces of hope and optimism to further implement the psychic life force within your higher mind.*

There is a positive, life-giving power in the emotion of hope and it tends to increase the levels of energy within the cells and maintains them in greater health than when the negative emotions of fear and worry are indulged.

Approach each day with this positive psychic emotion of hope. See the bright side to life, not the dark. See people as being good, not evil. Look for beauty, not ugliness. Indulge the emotion of hope regarding your person in daily affairs, and see the outcome always as positive, not negative. There is a chemistry to thought, and when you habitually indulge the emotion of hope, you will release the psychic life energy that causes the chemistry of your body to be alkaline not acid. The negative emotions tend to curtail the psychic life force of your higher mind and lower the body's resistance to the invasion of germs. This produces sickness.

4. *Try to express daily the positive emotion of happiness as this releases positive psychic power within your brain and body.*

A happy person is generally a healthy person. There is an amazing psychic life energy that this emotion of happiness releases to the body which maintains it in perfect health. Scientists experimented with groups of people who were given mental images of happiness, and told to relive their most happy experiences in their minds; then the chemicals of their bodies were tested and it was found that their bodies released sugar and other chemicals that gave them energy and a cheerful, happy outlook on life which produced vibrant good health.

Then these same people were told to think of the most unhappy incidents in their lives, and after dwelling on these negative thoughts for a while, tests were again taken of the body's chemistry. In every instance it was found that the glands poisoned the cells of the body, producing fatigue, lassitude, depression and melancholy.

5. *Release the psychic energy of the healing emotion of love in your daily conduct.*

It has been found that the emotion of love is one of the most creative, healing and constructive emotions that man can indulge. When you release the psychic energy of love in your daily life, you will live in a constant flow of psychic energy from the higher centers of your brain.

A case of arthritis healed

A woman I knew had crippling arthritis for years. She came into our lecture work in Carnegie Hall, and told me of her inability to find a cure for her condition. I knew there was some psychic and emotional reason for her problem and asked her to tell me about herself. She told me that twenty-five years before she had loved a man, who was going to marry her. Then her sister took this man away from her and married him. She hated her sister from that day on, and became a bitter, unforgiving spinster who lived in the emotion of hate.

After a period of five years or so, she began to develop the condition known as arthritis, and soon she was so crippled that she could hardly do her housework. For twenty years she tried every known diet and medical aid, but nothing helped her. When she told me that she had not seen nor spoken to her sister all during those years, I knew that she had been short-circuiting the psychic life centers which regulate the flow of life-energy and health within her body. I told her to write her sister, to forgive her, to try to understand her conduct, and love her once again.

This woman followed my advice, and soon she and her sister were back together again, united by the bonds of love and understanding. Within six months time the same psychic force that had produced the arthritis began to dissolve it within her body and she was able to use her hands more freely. Within a year or two, there was hardly a trace of swelling in her joints and no more pain.

6. *Life and psychic energy flow where there is a purpose in life.*

Ask yourself the question: What am I living for? Then answer truthfully. Are you living just to make money? Or to do good and to help others? To make people happy?

Psychic life force and energy flow from the higher psychic centers of your brain WHEN YOU LIVE FOR SOME HIGH AND WORTHY PURPOSE.

If you have a selfish desire to become rich for yourself alone, it is not as powerful a motivator for the life force as if you have a desire to educate your children, help your family attain a higher standard of living, or improve the world.

7. *Listen to the voice of psychic guidance within your own mind which tells you what is good for your health and what is destructive.*

A still small voice within man's higher psychic centers tells him what to eat and drink, and what to think to maintain perfect health. If man ignores this inner psychic guiding voice, he eats the wrong foods, drinks injurious poisons and pollutes his body with energy-killing materials that destroy him.

Something within your mind will tell you not to smoke, that it is injurious. The fact millions smoke does not make it right. Science now proves that it is injurious, but people smoke more than ever. This will to kill himself in man, is one of the most baffling problems which face sociologists and scientists. When man listens to this inner, guiding voice, he knows intuitively what to eat, how to exercise, how to breathe correctly, how to rest and restore his body's energy and how to live a natural, long life with perfect health.

Psychic warning could have saved this child

A child of five craved table salt and at mealtime she would open the salt shaker and take out a handful of salt and before anyone could stop her, put it into her mouth and swallow it. Her parents were horrified and tried to stop the little girl from doing this, as they feared it would be injurious to her health. The child persisted in trying to get salt into her system but the parents carefully watched her and denied her the salt she craved. A few weeks later the child developed a certain type of brain tumor which killed her. The grief-stricken parents found that only salt would have dissolved and healed the incipient tumor which killed the girl. Her higher psychic mind was trying to save her life.

8. *Follow the intuitive mind within in matters of diet and health.*

You can learn how to hear the divine promptings of your higher psychic mind within your brain and body cells, by following the intuitive guidance which it tries to give you in matters pertaining to diet. Should you be a vegetarian or a meat eater? Should you take vitamins and minerals? Should you have innoculations to safeguard you against colds, polio, and other ailments?

You and you alone can make the ultimate decision as to what is best for your health and life.

Follow your own intuition as to your diet and you will

not go wrong. Your higher mind will tell your body cells through cravings you have for certain types of food, what chemical your body needs at certain times, and you will be intuitively guided to seek out that type of food.

Scientists now say that children should not be forced to eat foods they do not like, such as spinach or bread, or any other food. If a child turns down milk for several days, a parent should not force him to drink it. Intuitively, the child will start to drink milk when his body needs it.

If ten foods are put before a child, he will instinctively select the foods his body needs at that time. I knew an instance of a child of six who craved bananas. He would not eat any other food for several days. His parents were frantic but they could not force him to eat anything else. A few days later the child asked for other food. His banana binge was over and his higher mind sent a message to his body cells to eat something else for a change.

9. *Have a purpose for living which encompasses high ideals and creativeness to implement the life force.*

The famous American, Grandma Moses, was frail and sickly at age seventy-five and people did not think she had long to live. She released the reserves of psychic energy within her brain and body with a desire to create beauty for the world. She began to paint pictures and soon the will to life and health flamed so strongly that she lived to be over a hundred and her paintings sold for thousands of dollars.

Cecil Rhodes went to Africa to die of tuberculosis, but the will to live reasserted itself when he discovered a diamond field, and he had a desire to do good with his money; he became healed and founded the Rhodes Scholarships, and lived out his natural life in good health. The psychic reserves of life and energy were stimulated by his will to live.

Jane Addams, who founded Hull House in Chicago, was sick and had only six months to live, when she began doing charitable work for children. She opened her home as a center and was so busy expressing the creative psychic will to help others that the life force once again flowed and she lived well past eighty.

32

The will to live, to be, to do, to create, to love—these are the psychic keys releasing vast reserves of life forces within the brain and body cells.

Summary of Chapter 1

1. The dynamic psychic power that resides within your brain and may be used for building health, energy and power.
2. How the psychic voice of the Cosmos speaks to your body cells giving them life energy.
3. How a man was brought back from death with psychic suggestions of life and health.
4. The five psychic mechanisms which can keep the body healthy and functional at all times.
5. Love—the psychic force that keeps your mind and body attuned to the cosmic rhythm of health.
6. A desire to help others that helped heal a woman of serious illness and brought her happiness and new life.
7. How to use the psychic regime for vibrant good health and long life.
8. How you can implement the psychic life force within your body through faith.
9. Hope and optimism, the positive emotions that stimulate psychic energy in your brain and body for good health.
10. How one woman was healed of arthritis by forgiving her sister whom she had hated for twenty-five years.
11. How a five-year-old child could have been saved from brain tumor if her parents had listened to psychic guidance.

chapter 2

How to Channel the
Invisible Psychic Powers
That Control Your Life

What is psychic power?

It is the ability to receive impressions, warnings and intuitive guidance from a higher mind that operates through the human psyche.

Psychic powers express themselves in many forms from hunches to clairvoyant dreams in which we often are warned of impending danger to ourselves or loved ones.

You can tap this invisible psychic power that controls your life and let it guide you to your right destiny.

You can learn secrets about others through this power.

You can be told whom to marry, how to overcome problems, how to develop gifts and talents, how to make a million dollars.

This psychic power is available to you every moment of the night and day when you are once aware of it.

There is a vast, underlying sea of Cosmic Intelligence in the universe which your mind may tap for psychic guidance. This Cosmic Intelligence pulsates throughout time and space in wavelengths that encompass all creation.

Your higher psychic centers, when attuned to this Cosmic Mind, can channel its power through your mind and project it to your body, your environment, and to other people, shaping and molding your life according to the cosmic blueprint which fits your particular destiny.

You may use the invisible laws of psychic phenomena to communicate with other minds at will. This invisible sea of intelligence connects all human beings with the cosmos, and there is a vast system of cosmic communication between all the cells in the universal body.

Just as your radio and television sets may receive wavelengths of sounds and pictures from outer space, so too, your higher psychic centers, when correctly attuned to the cosmic mind, may receive psychic guidance and intuition.

THE MYSTICAL COSMIC VOICE SPEAKS TO YOU

There is a mystical cosmic voice which can speak to you in the innermost secret places of your being. Man's mind is more than a conscious, volitional, creative intelligence. It has a higher dimension, and through the superconscious mind you may have all knowledge, all power for every purpose of your life.

You are a creative force in your own right. You may use creative psychic power to shape the life of your choice. You can tap the psychic power of the Cosmic Memory bank of the universe and draw to yourself the guiding intelligence which can cause you to build anything you desire for your future destiny.

There are invisible laws that exist in the Cosmos which determine how all creation shall operate. Your mind has within its confines all the necessary knowledge and power to draw upon the Cosmic Mind of the universe and obtain any portion of that intelligence which you may require to live your life fully.

Through psychic fusion of your mind with the Cosmic Mind, you may create a powerful medium through which divine intuition will flow into your life and lead you to stupendous achievement.

You can enter the innermost stillness of your soul, where this divine power resides, and find the pattern for anything you choose. You may still your own conscious mind and receive divine guidance, instruction, or even warnings of how to avert danger.

HOW LETTERS OF FIRE
WARNED A WOMAN OF DANGER

A lady I once knew, who was very intuitive and psychic, was planning a trip to Europe with her husband to see his family. One day, as she sat quietly in her living room, meditating, she suddenly saw written on the wall, in letters of fire, these words:

Do not take this trip: there is danger.

She told her husband of the psychic message she had received, and begged him to cancel the trip. He scoffed at the idea of danger and, as he had not seen his relatives for some years, he insisted they take the trip. They went to England, despite her objections, and she had an accident that crippled her and paralyzed her legs for life!

If this lady had listened to this warning voice, which came in the form of written words, she could have been spared.

HOW YOU CAN BEGIN TO USE PSYCHIC POWER

You can begin to use psychic power immediately, when you understand some of the invisible laws that pertain to this study. As light waves work under certain universal laws, so too, psychic and intuitive powers work under cosmic laws which are as definite as the laws of gravity or electricity.

The general field of psychical research in which scientists as well as laymen are working to confirm the facts of psychic phenomena, is known as extrasensory perception, and abbreviated ESP.

Your usual perceptions are received through your five senses: sight, smell, hearing, touch and taste. These are said to be sensory in nature, that is, pertaining to the physical body and the physical organism known as the brain.

However, psychic powers are concerned with perceptions received through other than the ordinary five senses and are said to be extra—meaning outside of the usual sensory perceptions. Sometimes these higher intuitive functions are called: intuition, hunches, premonitions, visions, psychic dreams, precognition, clairvoyance, clairaudience, mental telepathy, astral projections and psychometry.

The scientific study of these extrasensory perceptions has been termed the science of parapsychology.

Psychology deals with the nature of human and animal behavior and science knows a great deal about this realm of behavior. Parapsychology deals with the realm of the invisible, sometimes called the fourth dimension, and goes beyond the boundaries of psychology, into the mystic realm, where mind is more than a mere emanation of a physical brain.

YOU CAN TAP THE WORLD OF THE INVISIBLE

You have the power to tap this vast world of the invisible, in which exist all forms of power and intelligence. You can do this by entering the psychic realm of spirit and meditating on the highest concepts that man may know. You can then channel this Cosmic Intelligence into your own mind and experience and receive psychic pictures, telepathic communications, thought waves and intuitive knowledge such as the great geniuses of all time have received.

HOW A MOTHER
RECEIVED A PSYCHIC WARNING

Mothers, who are closer to their children spiritually and emotionally than others, often receive psychic impulses which relate to their children or other members of their family.

A woman of my acquaintance, who had never had any definite psychic impressions before, had a five-month-old son, and one day she left him in care of a baby-sitter while she went to a woman's club to play bridge. After playing about an hour, this woman had a terrible feeling that something was wrong with her baby. She kept telling herself that it was ridiculous, as she knew the baby-sitter was taking care of her child and would have called her if anything were wrong. She tried to disodge the uneasy feeling from her mind, but she couldn't. She felt a sense of suffocation and, unable to restrain her fears any longer, she rushed to a telephone and called her home. There was no answer.

Now really frantic, she rushed to her home, which was fortunately only a short distance away, and found that the baby-sitter was not there. She ran into her son's room and saw that he had become entangled in his bedclothes and was literally suffocating! If she had not responded to the psychic warning she received her child would surely have died. She found out later that the baby-sitter had grown bored with her task and had gone out for a walk around the block!

WHAT MENTAL TELEPATHY MEANS

The words "mental telepathy" mean the ability of one mind to transmit or receive from another mind over a distance, some kind of message. "Tele" means transmitting, and "pathy" refers to feeling or emotion between two people. Usually it is during times of emergency or great danger that the human mind or spirit is able to transmit some form of spiritual energy, like radioactive waves, which reach the sensitized areas of the other person's mind, making him aware of the loved one's danger.

How often a mother of a soldier experiences a psychic vision or feeling that her son has died! This often happens at the exact moment of the boy's death. I know of a woman who had a son in the South Pacific. One night she awakened from a very disturbing dream in which she saw her son being shot down over the ocean. A few days later she received a message from the War Department telling her that her son's airplane had been shot down by an enemy plane. She later learned that it had happened at the same time she had her horrible psychic dream!

HOW A WOMAN HAD PSYCHIC PREMONITION OF HER HUSBAND'S DANGER

Another woman I know had a feeling of dreadful constriction in her chest upon hearing her telephone ring.

She had a premonition that something had happened to her husband. The man's voice at the other end of the line said, "Your husband has been injured in a truck and car collision and is at the hospital. Come quickly." He gave her the name of the hospital and hung up. The woman went to the emergency ward and found that her husband had been crushed in a car by a ten-ton truck and had suffered serious chest injuries!

HOW TO TAP THE POWER OF PSYCHIC PHENOMENA

1. Go into a state of silent meditation, where you remove all thoughts from your conscious mind. Sit in a room by yourself, and be sure that you are not disturbed during this period of meditation.

2. Say over and over to yourself, "Peace, be still. Be still, be still." Then visualize your mind like a calm, peaceful lake, in which there are no ripples on the surface. When the lake of your mind is tranquil and calm it may reflect the intelligence that is in the Cosmic Memory bank of the universe, which possesses all secrets and which ties all human beings together in invisible wavelengths.

3. Now you are ready to begin the process of receiving thought forms or messages from the cosmos. Enter into the state of consciousness we call psychic somnambulism —meaning, to feel as if you are about to enter into a state of sleep. You conscious mind will feel lethargic and sleepy, but one part of your mind will be fully awake and in a state of *knowing* and *awareness*. It is this part of consciousness, which I call the mirrorscope of the soul, which will reflect from the Cosmic Memory bank the information that you wish, or that gives you psychic pictures and messages.

4. Let thoughts or pictures float into your mind *without conscious effort on your part* and you will begin to receive a whole series of impressions. Some of these will be in the form of symbols or pictures; others will come as thoughts, some may flow through your higher mind like a stream of consciousness giving you words, sentences, names, dates,

or impressions of places. You will generally receive psychic impressions in keeping with your particular needs, your emotional state, and your deep personal concerns. Sometimes these impressions will come as emotional states; a feeling of danger relating to someone you know; a feeling of exultation about some happy experience that projects on the mirror of your mind; or it may be a warning to be cautious of some person you have just met, or an idea how you can make money through writing a song, a story, or inventing some device.

5. Try to remember the impressions that come fleeting through your consciousness. *Do not make any effort to control them at this stage,* but let them flicker in the sensitive areas of your mind like motion pictures upon a screen.

6. If there is some specific information you want to know as you sit in this state of psychic somnambulism, ask the question of the Cosmic Intelligence, quietly, speaking to yourself. You might frame it in this way: "Should I take the trip I plan to Europe?" It may be some information regarding a business move; "Should I go into business with Frank at this time?" Or it may be some emotional problem about which you wish information. "Does Mary really love me and should I marry her?"

7. After you have asked the specific question let your mind remain completely blank, and then wait for the answer to come. Sometimes the information will come as impressions, and you may believe that your own conscious mind is giving you the answer to your question. However, as you have suspended you own conscious volitional mind in the process of psychic somnambulism, and you are in a half-waking and half-dreaming state, it is more likely that your super-conscious mind is giving you the answers, and generally correct ones.

Do not be afraid to trust this higher mind, for when you practice and use this power daily, you will begin to have more confidence in this psychic power and use your conscious mind less and less. The answer may come to you as a definite message couched in words, such as: "No, do not take the trip to Europe, for this is a time of danger and complication and you will be better off not going on a trip at this time," or, "Yes, go into the business deal with Frank. He is honest and trustworthy and you will make money." Or it may state, "This is not the time for you to marry. You can find a girl who is more sincere than Mary, and you would be better off waiting until you meet her."

8. After you receive your psychic response and you come out of your psychic somnambulance, jot down some of your psychic impressions, with the date of your sitting, so you can check them later against the events that transpire.

9. To more forcibly imprint your requests and questions upon the higher intelligence within you, which gives you the specific answers, you may go into your psychic meditation sessions with questions or requests already written down. Then all you need do is hold your conscious mind perfectly still, like a reflecting mirror and let it record the fleeting impressions that arise in your consciousness. Sometimes your answers to your questions will come from your higher consciousness in the form of stream of consciousness, in which the first person singular, "I," is substituted for the second person singular, "You." You must be careful to distinguish between your own conscious mind's promptings, and the super-conscious mind's. Your conscious mind is apt to couch things in terms of what you personally desire, whereas your super-conscious mind will often send thoughts that are contrary to your personal desires and preferences.

10. Try not to sit in psychic meditation for more than one hour at a time at first, for the mind may grow restless and begin to wander if you persist in sitting too long. Later, when you have become more proficient in the art of psychic reflection, you can sit for two hours or even longer, without any harm to your conscious mind. Many authors, painters and creative artists, inventors and scientists who are under psychic inspiration, can work for hours at a time without tiring. This art of psychic meditation can restore energy, and release high inspiration and creative power into your conscious mind that will carry you on to new heights of mental and physical power.

41

Summary of Chapter 2

1. How you may tap the sea of Cosmic Intelligence and use it for your every need.
2. The Cosmic Memory bank in which all secrets are stored.
3. The silent voice that speaks to man.
4. The invisible forces that work miracles in the universe.
5. How to tap the radiatory wavelengths that create all living things in the universe.
6. The psychic blueprint that you may use for greater creative power.
7. How to use phychic fusion to tap the Cosmic Mind that can help shape your destiny.
8. How a psychic warning could have saved a woman from an accident if she had listened to it.
9. Extrasensory perception as a sixth sense which you may cultivate as you do your other senses.
10. How to tap the world of the invisible and discover all forms of intelligence and new, dynamic power.
11. A child's life saved when his mother received and obeyed a psychic warning that her child was in danger.
12. How you can use mental telepathy to receive messages from other minds, and how to send psychic messages to others.
13. The regime for tapping the realm of psychic phenomena which will enable you to utilize the tremendous powers of your higher psychic centers.

chapter 3

How to Communicate
with Others Through
Psychic Telepathy

You have the power to direct messages to other people through a force that is similar to telegraphy.

You also have the ability to receive psychic messages from other people by attuning your brain wavelengths to them and listening to the subtle, psychic voices that are in the air all about you.

Psychic telepathy can also put you in touch with the invisible vibrations of those who have lived in past ages and have gone on to another dimension of time and space.

This power is known as psychic telepathy.

All psychic phenomena are based on laws that control vibration and invisible wavelengths in the universe. You have the power to communicate with others through psychic telepathy. Your mind perceives the physical and material universe through your five senses and physical wavelengths give us color, form and sensation. There is a sixth sense in your subconscious which gives you an awareness of higher psychic impulses which travel through time and space as electrical and magnetic vibrations.

Light travels at a speed of one hundred and eighty-six thousand miles per second. Electricity travels at an even greater speed; thought waves, which are electrical in nature, travel at billions of miles per second and can circle the globe faster than light.

YOUR MIND A RECEIVING AND SENDING
STATION

Your mind is like a radio receiving and sending station, capable of transmitting thoughts to other minds, or able to receive the thoughts that are in the atmosphere which others are trying to communicate to you. You may even tune in on thoughts that are NOT directed specifically at you, but which circulate in the atmosphere as electrical impulses or emotional thought forms. Many people have picked up similar ideas for inventions, songs, stories and movie scripts, from these thought waves and later found that another person, in another part of the world, also tuned in on the same wavelength and received the same idea.

As a radio or television sending station depends on electrical impulses to transmit its sounds and forms, so too the human psyche depends on mental and electrical impulses to send its thought forms to other minds or to receive them. Just as you can tune in on a certain station to receive a particular program, so too your higher mind can be tuned in on thought currents, thought forms, emotional impulses, and psychic symbols which can be interpreted by your mind.

WHAT IS MENTAL TELEPATHY?

There are two forms of projecting and receiving mental and psychic impulses: one is through *mental* telepathy, the other through *psychic* telepathy. Mental telepathy deals with the sending of thoughts and messages to others through specific words such as: "John, telephone me. It is urgent. Phone me at once. It is an emergency." These words, repeated over and over, charged with emotional energy, can be projected to the person one wishes to reach, and he may feel a vague sense of unrest, an urge to telephone his home without knowing why.

An example of how this form of mental telepathy worked was the case of a woman I once knew whose child was very sick. Her husband was on the road as a salesman, and she was desperate to reach him. She sat quietly for fifteen or twenty minutes saying his name several times, and then repeating to herself the words: "Phil, call me at once. Gina is very sick. It is an emergency. Phone me, Phil, phone me at once."

Within two hours this woman's phone rang and her husband said, "I had a terrible restless urge to phone you. Is something wrong?" She told him of their daughter's illness and he rushed home by plane immediately.

We all know of instances where this form of mental telepathy worked to warn someone to do a certain thing at a certain time. Many times the thought will not lodge in the other person's mind immediately; he may be preoccupied, or his conscious mind may be so active that he cannot receive the telepathic communications. As the percipient, the one receiving the psychic message, must be in a receptive state, it very often happens that a message does not get through on time. Moments of reverie, daydreaming, or sleepiness, are best for receiving such projected telepathic messages. Even when we are asleep the higher mind often receives and registers these telepathic communications from other minds and they are then projected into the dream state. Sometimes these projections are actual prophecies of events to occur, other times they are communications with other minds that are projecting wavelengths that lodge in our own minds through the universal law of magnetic attraction.

PSYCHIC TELEPATHY
DEALS WITH THOUGHT FORMS

Psychic telepathy is different from mental telepathy in that it deals with though forms and symbols rather than actual words. Words are symbols of an emotional thought form we wish to express. The word "money" is in reality a symbol of comfort, home, automobiles, material goods, security, and other values. Very often your mind will receive symbols instead of direct words or messages, and it is essential that you understand these psychic symbols and interpret them correctly. The symbol of marriage is a wedding band. The same symbol might come through telepathically for love. A boat is a symbol of travel; so is a train or an airplane. Very often a telepathic message will come through in the form of a symbol instead of the word. These symbols most often come through in dreams, but very often they come through while we are in a passive state, thinking of nothing in particular, when the symbol will flash upon the screen of the mind vividly.

A symbolism of roses

A man I once knew dreamed that he presented a beautiful bouquet of red roses to a girl whose face he could not see. He felt a strong romantic urge towards this girl, and it disturbed him because he could not see her face. A few weeks later, at a social function, he was introduced to a girl named Rose, and he felt an instant magnetic attraction to her. It was only when he had proposed marriage to her some weeks later that he realized Rose was the unknown girl of his dreams symbolized by the red roses.

What a boat symbolized

Another instance in which psychic telepathy predicted a future event for a lady I know, was a dream she often had in which she saw a giant ocean liner like the Queen Mary, which was taking her to Europe. She had no particular desire to travel, but four months later she had an opportunity to go to London by plane, and she realized that her prophetic dream, symbolized by a boat, was an indication of an impending event.

HOW TO SEND PSYCHIC MESSAGES TO OTHERS

You can deliberately select the persons you wish to reach through mental and psychic telepathy. You can project these psychic messages in direct words, or in emotional states, or through psychic symbols.

1. Go into the silence by repeating some mystical phrase, such as the Tibetan *AUM MANE PADME AUM,* several times. Or you might say, from the Bible, PEACE, BE STILL, AND KNOW THAT I AM GOD. Or you

might repeat the twenty-third Psalm. When your mind is in a perfect state of stillness, you are ready to begin the process of projecting psychic messages to others through telepathy.

2. Breathe deeply ten or fifteen times to generate the personal electrical power you will require to project your messages. Remember, your mind is electrical and magnetic in nature, and works under the same laws that electricity does. To become a sending station telepathically, you must generate a great deal of power.

3. Close your eyes and go into a dreamy, half-sleeping, half-waking state, where your conscious mind is still. Do not worry about anything during this stage, otherwise it will disturb the psychic vibrations you are trying to project.

4. Choose the person you wish to communicate with psychically. See his face clearly, or if you have a picture, look at the picture before going into your psychic silence.

5. Emotionalize the thought you are trying to send. If it is a person whom you are trying to help, feel a *deep emotion* of love and hold in your mind the thought that you are trying to help the person.

Example of penetrating emotion

Mrs. G. had a husband who drank excessively. He would become vicious if she mentioned his drinking to him. She tried using this method of psychic telepathy to reach her husband's higher mind. She wanted him to stop drinking and gambling all his money away. She sat in daily sessions of half an hour, and held his face in the forefront of her mind. Then she breathed deeply, and put her mind into psychic communication, as she said his name over and over. "John, you will listen to me. You will change for the sake of our love and that of our children. You will stop your drinking and gambling. You will see that it is ruining our lives. I love you, John, and want you to love me like you did when we were first married."

Mrs. G. kept up these psychic sessions for several weeks. She *stopped nagging* her husband, began loving him more, and sending out wavelengths of love and forgiveness. Soon her husband noticed the change in her personality; he remarked about it one day. "What's hap-. pened to you? You don't nag like you used to." Mrs. G. kept up her psychic suggestions and within three weeks' time her husband began to stay home more often, and soon began to drink less and less. Her nagging and demands in the past made him rebellious and vindictive. Now, with her changed attitude, her husband's psychic response centers began to operate on wavelengths of love and kindness, and he could not continue in his destructive habits. Soon Mrs. G's husband stopped drinking and gambling, and showed every indication that his higher psychic centers, *without being aware of it* had received his wife's psychic promptings which he implicitly obeyed.

6. Practice projecting messages in direct statements and words to people you select to communicate with psychically, and then also practice sending thought forms and symbols, *by concentrating on thoughts and thought forms rather than words.*

7. You can also project thought forms of pictures you cut out of magazines—cars, houses, furniture, television sets, pianos, jewelry, fur coats—anything that you wish to form psychic images of and project to the outer world. It will be magnetized and contact some person or persons who can bring you the fulfillment of your projected desires.

A psychic projection of a home

An example of how this type of psychic projection works is that of a lady who attended my lectures and classes in New York City. She projected the psychic thought form of a home she wanted to buy in the country. She cut out pictures of the house she wanted, furnished it from home magazines, and each day concentrated her psychic thought forms and projected them to the outer world. *She did not know who would make it possible for her to achieve the fulfillment of her psychic dream home,* but she had faith that it would happen somehow. One day she went into town on business; she saw a sign announcing lottery tickets for sale. She had a psychic hunch to buy one, the first time she had done so. When the names were drawn for the big prizes, this woman drew a prize of fifty thousand dollars! Her dream home came to her, through a channel she could never have guessed.

Other types of psychic projection

You can project the thought form of the man or woman you wish to attract for a future mate, and hold in mind the qualities you desire, and that thought form will lodge in the mind of such a person who will be magnetically attracted to you.

You can project psychic thought forms to those close to you whom you wish to change for the better. A mother had a sixteen-year-old son who had taken to smoking. She kept telling him in her daily psychic sessions: "Bill, you will stop smoking. It is injurious to your health. You will begin to feel that cigarettes taste bitter and you will give up this harmful, destructive habit. I want you to grow into a strong, healthy man, and you will stop smoking at once."

This woman reported to me that within three weeks' time her son Bill began to tell her that he had less of an urge to smoke. After a meal one day, he stopped smoking, crushed out his cigarette and said, "I don't know why, but this cigarette tastes bitter! I'm going to swear off cigarettes from now on, mom." He never touched another cigarette from that day on!

SECRETS OF TELEPATHIC HYPNOSIS

It is possible to use the projection of telepathic hypnosis to reach the minds of others and cause them to do your bidding. Just as a hypnotist can give suggestions to a subject and cause him to do certain things, so too, you can project psychic thought forms, words and messages to the minds of those you select, imprinting these psychic suggestions upon their sensitive higher psychic centers. How-

49

ever, if you send out negative, destructive, or immoral telepathic suggestions the other person's psychic neuro-response centers will automatically reject them.

THE FOUR STEPS TO TAKE FOR TELEPATHIC HYPNOSIS

1. It is important that you be emotionally close to the person you are trying to influence through telepathic hypnosis. A husband, wife, father or mother; any relative who is close to you, is already connected to you by psychic wavelengths, which make it possible for you to communicate psychically. You cannot project telepathic suggestions to a person you hate, or that you want to hurt. You must sincerely have a desire to help the person achieve some positive, worthwhile goal, for psychic vibrations are in the same realm of spiritual and soul impulses. Good will work miracles; so will love, and a desire to help others.

2. In your projection sessions of telepathic hypnosis hold the face of the person you are trying to reach in your mind's eye. Project a golden line for communication like an umbilical or mystic cord between your forehead and the contemplated forehead of the other person. As you give your positive suggestions see them travelling over this golden mystic cord to the other person's brain centers. As you give your suggestions breathe deeply several times and project your words as you project your breath. It is best to speak the suggestion aloud, in a firm, commanding voice, at the same time projecting the breath and the golden line of infinity.

3. Use positive words and commands, such as:

John, you will hear my suggestions and act on them. I want you to overcome your bad habit of gambling and spending money. You will begin to save money and stop spending it foolishly. I love you and want to save our marriage. You will receive these positive suggestions and act upon them at once.

4. It is important that you repeat the suggestions over and over, at least ten to twenty times. You can word the message just as you would if you were talking to the person. If you are in a place where you cannot say the suggestions aloud, you can whisper them to yourself and, as the thoughts are electrical in nature, they will still radiate in the atmosphere and be magnetically attracted to the person you are projecting to.

How hypnotic telepathy healed marital infidelity

An example of how this form of hypnotic telepathy works is that of a woman whom I once knew who found out that her husband was seeing another woman. Her first temptation was to have it out with her husband and leave him. She had studied psychic phenomena and knew many of these secrets of the higher mind. She began this process of talking the entire problem over with her husband psychically. She instructed him to give up his immoral ways, told him of her deep love for him, and suggested that he and the other woman stop seeing each other.

One night, just three weeks from the time she began her suggestions, this woman was lying in bed beside her husband. He was breathing deeply and she thought he was already asleep. Suddenly he spoke, and his voice, she later told me, sounded like one in a trance. He told her the entire story about the other woman and wound up by saying, "I am terribly sorry for having hurt you this way. I still love you and only you. I'll never see her again." He was true to his word, and this couple went on to a happier relationship than they had ever known before.

HOW YOU MAY RECEIVE PSYCHIC TELEPATHY FROM OTHERS

The psychic and telepathic centers of your higher mind are like a motion picture camera and projector; they are capable of registering thought forms and messages from the minds of others and they are also capable of projecting thought forms and psychic impulses to the minds of other people.

In trying to receive psychic thought forms and messages, the same principle applies; first you must attune your mind to the person you are trying to receive messages from, and you must concentrate your mind exclusively on that person, not shift your mind from one person to another.

THE RULES FOR PSYCHIC RECEPTION

1. Still your mind, just as in the instructions for sending psychic messages, by repeating over and over, "Peace, be still. Be still and know that I am God." Sit with your eyes gently closed, in as relaxed a manner as possible. If there is any tension in your mind or body it is apt to interfere with the reception of psychic impulses. Feel that you are in a half-sleeping state, where your mind feels dreamy and hazy.

2. Generate power for receiving psychic impulses by doing the same deep breathing you did for sending psychic messages. Electricity is the power which the higher psychic nerve centers use in transmitting messages, and it is the same power which you use in receiving psychic impulses. Deep, diaphragmatic breathing is suggested, with a count of four for the indrawn breath, then a count of four, while the breath is held, and a count of four as the breath is released.

3. Put yourself into a positive, restful emotional state by playing soft music in the background. You can have a candle lit, instead of the harsh glare of electric lights, and there can be incense burning or perfume, to give a relaxing, pleasant fragrance to help unlock the higher receptive centers of the brain. (This is one reason why in churches they often have candle light, incense burning and other aids to help release the higher spiritual and psychic centers from the inhibiting influence of harsh reality in the outer world.)

4. Mentally tune in on the person's wavelength that you wish to contact. See his face clearly in your mind's eye.

Say his name over several times. Ask questions or make statements just as you would if you were talking to the person face to face. You might ask specific questions if you wish information about something, such as: "Will you help me in this new business venture?" or, "Can you advance me the money I need?" or, "Are you sincere in your love for me?"

Then after asking the question or questions, sit quietly and *let* psychic impulses come into your mind. You have set up thought currents that are vibrating in the wavelengths of the other person's mind, and you will receive some response of either thoughts he has had about some subject, or specific answers to your own questions.

5. As you hold the person's face in your mind's eye, all kinds of thoughts about that person will begin to flood your mind. How will you know what part of your reception of thought forces is imagination on your part and what is authentic? It may take quite a good deal of practice in the art of psychic reception and transmission to separate the wheat from the chaff. Gradually the psychic selector within your mind will begin to tell you *when* you are correctly attuned to the other person's thought waves, and that you are in a state of psychic and telepathic communication.

How this psychic power worked a family reconciliation

Martha M. was a member of my lecture group in New York's Carnegie Hall. She had been estranged from her father for about ten years because she had married a man the father did not approve of. This man deserted Martha and her baby. The father was quite well off, and wrote Martha that he was cutting her off in his will and leaving the entire estate to her brother.

One day, while sitting in a psychic state of receptivity under my guidance, which she did as a daily habit, Martha suddenly saw a vision of her father's face; he was pale and thin and looked sick. She got the definite impression that her father was in a hospital. She received a psychic impulse to write him a letter, telling him she was sorry for their misunderstanding and that she still loved him dearly and wanted to be with him once again.

Martha's father received her letter and was so touched by her expression of love that he wrote her, forgiving her and asking for her forgiveness. He was sick and in a hospital, just as Martha had seen him to be in her psychic vision. The doctors gave him only a short time to live.

Martha took a plane the next day to the West Coast to see her father and they had a complete reconciliation. A few weeks later her father died, but before doing so, he changed his will, leaving Martha a fortune of more than a hundred thousand dollars!

6. You can also ask for specific information from the Cosmic Memory bank of the universe, where billions of psychic impulses and thoughts are stored, and receive ideas and thought forms for inventions, stories, songs, chemical formulas, as well as information about new business ventures or investments in the stock market.

Telepathic reception for investment information

Several members of my New York lecture group use this system of telepathic reception for information about the stock market. One man kept getting the symbol of a ringing bell in his psychic sessions. He was asking for information on how to invest his money. At first he thought the psychic message coming through was about the Bell Telephone Company, but he kept searching through lists of stocks until he came across the name Packard Bell, which was selling for about nine dollars a share. He felt a sense of rightness about this stock, for his psychic selector instantly signalled him this was it. He bought one thousand shares of this stock, held it for some months, and as it had gone into the forties when he sold it, made a profit of thousands!

7. Sometimes, while you sit in these psychic sessions no specific thought forms or messages will come through and you may feel that the vagrant ideas, symbols or pictures which float through your mind, are worthless. However, you should scrutinize them carefully, as the man

did who got the ringing bell, and you should write them down, for they may carry the germ of a symbolic idea which will be important to your future or present life.

8. Many times these psychic and telepathic messages and thought forms will come through in clairvoyant dreams. When you receive such information, and awaken, you should write down the vivid dream and let it serve to remind you in the future if the event occurs.

How doubting a clairvoyant dream cost Peter big winnings

A young man in Hollywood, Peter B., had such a psychic dream and it brought him a sum of money which he badly needed in his growing business. He dreamed two nights in a row that he was at the races at Santa Anita and the number one came up on the daily double for the first and second races. He was not a gambler, but the dream was so vivid that he decided to take one hundred dollars the next day and play the daily double on number one.

When Peter got to the daily double window to put down his hundred dollars on the number one combination, his conscious mind intruded and said, "Oh, don't be a fool! It was only a dream." He backed down on his original intentions and only bet twenty dollars on number one. As you may have guessed, his psychic dream proved accurate; he got his thirty-five hundred dollars, *but if he had followed his original psychic impulse to bet one hundred dollars,* he could have won a great deal more as the horses were both long shots!

9. Take into your practice sessions for psychic reception or projection, ideas that you write down previously. Hold each idea in your mind for a few moments and practice receiving as much information about the idea as you can get. You might write on such a slip of paper:

Should I go to Florida to live?
How can I make the thousand dollars I need to pay my bills?
Should I marry this girl, or wait until I meet someone else?

Should I trust this man to go into business?
What should I do about this health problem?
Should I buy a home at this time or wait longer?
How can I solve this problem?

As you hold each thought in your mind, let your mind remain passive and reflective. See what ideas come into your conscious mind.

Summary of Chapter 3

1. The laws ruling psychic phenomena and how to use them.
2. How to become a psychic receiving and sending station.
3. Mental and psychic telepathy and how you can use both forms to send and receive communications.
4. How to practice psychic silence for better psychic communication.
5. The secret of projecting psychic thought forms to other persons.
6. How psychic messages are often cloaked in symbols which come in reverie or in dreams.
7. Some common psychic symbols which you can interpret and use for psychic communication.
8. The regime for sending psychic messages to others.
9. How to use telepathic hypnosis to win others to your way of thinking.
10. Steps you can take to practice telepathic hypnosis.
11. How you can become a psychic receiving station for the thoughts and suggestions of other minds.

chapter 4

How to Contact the
Psychic Storehouse of
Cosmic Memory
for Perfect Guidance

You can be guided by higher psychic power to your right work or activities.

You can be shown how to find love-happiness in your life.

You can build a fortune and know security by following the psychic impulses of your higher mind.

You can receive secret information for building a business, developing a great creative talent, discovering a new formula, or inventing a great object like the telephone, radio, electric light or typewriter—*these images are all in the great storehouse of Cosmic Memory*—waiting for you to tap and channelize in your own mind.

There is an amazing flow of psychic intelligence in the cosmic realm which guides and controls man. It is in the psychic storehouse of Cosmic Memory that all creative ideas are stored. Here, in an invisible Cosmic Memory bank there exists the universal blueprint for creating everything we see in the entire universe. It is in this cosmic memory bank that all secrets, chemical formulas, atomic energy—everything that man requires for his growth and development—are stored in a vast psychic computer-like system which man's mind may tap and channelize for his own purposes. Perfect guidance in every department of his life is possible when man learns how to contact this psychic storehouse of memory for daily living.

HOW TO MAKE CONTACT THROUGH
PSYCHIC MIND CENTERS

It is through your higher psychic mind centers that you may contact this Cosmic Memory bank of the universe and channelize any portion of its knowledge, power and abundance for your own personal use. Everything in the future already exists in this Cosmic Memory bank, just waiting to be used!

You can discover the formula for personal happiness through this psychic guidance from your higher mind. Many people today are well-off, but there are more feelings of insecurity and threatening disaster than in any other comparable age. This gives rise to worry, fear and other unhealthy emotions. More millions are in mental hospitals than ever before; our young people are threatened with the spectres of crime, dope addiction, mental illness and immorality.

How to achieve true serenity and power

You can learn from this psychic intelligence how to achieve mental and emotional balance in a world that seems to have suddenly gone mad. You can discover your own hidden potentials for peace and happiness; you can balance your moods, control your temper and overcome the bad habits that might destroy your mental and physical health. Within the Cosmic Memory bank of the universe is the hidden, secret life force, which you may tap and channelize. You will be assured of vital energy, youth and power throughout your entire life, when you tap this unlimited reservoir of psychic intelligence. You will never fear old age, for this cosmic power does not fail a hundred-year-old oak tree any more than it does one that is only five years old.

You can discover and use the gift of psychic prophecy and know the events of your future through the Cosmic Memory, which tells a caterpillar how to become transformed into a winged butterfly, or which can turn a shapeless polliwog into a frog in a few days' time. This is a mystery that baffles the conscious mind of man, but to the psychic intelligence of the universe it is an everyday occurrence.

How to become a creative genius

You can become a creative genius by tapping the countless millions of forms, designs and intricate colorations that this Cosmic Memory bank contains. See how artistically this intelligence traces the lace-like leaves of a fern, or the geometric design of a snowflake. View the subtle shadings of a pink or red rose, with its velvety texture and its elusive fragrance, and know that you are witnessing a cosmic miracle in nature. See how wondrously this psychic intelligence spins out of the Cosmic Memory bank, the gossamer, iridescent wings of a humming bird and causes it to intelligently build its nest, and extract nectar through its elongated beak to nourish itself and its young.

How to find lost articles

You can use this psychic power in the storehouse of Cosmic Memory to guide you to the finding of lost articles, for this *Cosmic Mind never loses anything;* it is aware, through a vast, psychic computer-like system, of the location of every atom, every element, every object and every form that it has created since the beginning of time. When you misplace an object, this higher psychic power can lead you to its location.

You can also tap this Cosmic Memory bank, as countless thousands have, to find hidden treasures; to locate gold, silver, uranium or diamond fields. You can create new forms of matter, such as nylon and rayon, or new vegetables and fruits, such as Burbank did, or you may discover treasures in the sea or under the earth, if you can tune in on these hidden cosmic wavelengths in the universe.

HOW PSYCHIC GUIDANCE LED A PERSON TO A GOLD MINE!

One man who used this psychic power to find a gold mine in Nevada, was led to the exact location where he felt a huge deposit of gold was under the earth. Without previous mining experience, and only with his psychic guidance to lead him, he began to dig, and soon unearthed five million dollars in gold.

HOW TO BUILD YOUR FAITH IN THE COSMIC MIND POWER

Before you are able to receive the higher psychic pulsations of the Cosmic Mind that rules the universe, you must have a superabundance of faith in this power. It is an infinite intelligence that is inherent in every atom and cell of the entire universe.

The Cosmic Mind power holds the formulas that make up the atomic composition of all matter.

In the Cosmic Memory bank, which you will learn to tap through psychic mediumship for solving problems, there is all wisdom and knowledge leading to fame, fortune, and satisfying serenity.

How Cosmic Knowledge works in nature

When a beaver wants the knowledge to build a dam, it does not go to school to learn the laws of mathematics or architecture. It turns to this higher Cosmic Mind and receives instantaneously the knowledge for cutting the trees to the right size, for dragging them to the site of the dam and for packing mud into the crevices between the pieces of wood. It generally chooses an ideal location, the narrowest in the stream at which to build its dam.

When the honey bee wants to build its nest and store its

60

food for its young, it turns to this higher, Cosmic Mind and through psychic mediumship on its plane of consciousness, knows enough to build a six-sided cone out of wax, because it will store more honey than a five-sided cone.

The caterpillar weaves its cocoon and goes into a deep sleep, using the Cosmic Mind guidance to change from a crawling creature into a glorious, golden-winged butterfly.

A crawling beetle in the mud in the bottom of the lake has cosmic guidance which turns it into a dragonfly with iridescent wings and seventeen hundred eyes! Truly a miracle of psychic transfiguration which no ordinary mind could perform.

Tiny ants build vast colonies, cultivate crops, have herds of plant lice as "cows" and know how to survive through this Cosmic Mind type of guidance.

The chameleon has protective camouflage to conceal it from its enemies. This secret power is given to many creatures in nature, like the squid and octopus, which are able to eject an inky stream when attacked to confuse their enemies.

The armadillo, tortoise and porcupine have protective shells and spiny armour to ward off the attacks of their enemies. No ordinary mentality could devise such fantastic natural endowments as these or the thick skin of the elephant, rhinoceros or hippopotamus. Yet, to the Cosmic Intelligence which created these wonders this is ordinary, every-day creative procedure which it performs with the greatest of ease.

The Cosmic Intelligence of you

As if all these creative miracles of Cosmetic Mind were not enough, stop for a moment and think of the greatest miracle of all; you, a human being, created in nine short months' time with a brain, heart, lungs, eyes that see, ears that hear, and a consciousness that makes you aware of the miracle you truly are.

THE STEPS YOU MAY TAKE
TO CONTACT THE FABULOUS
PSYCHIC STOREHOUSE OF COSMIC MEMORY

1. You should choose a room for these psychic sessions where you will be undisturbed for at least one to two hours daily. You can have soft lights and music. Put yourself into a contemplative mood, with your body in a restful position, either sitting up or lying down. You will try to lull your conscious mind into a state between sleeping and waking. It is best to have your eyes gently closed during these periods of psychic reception.

2. You can have a sheet of paper with you for some of the practice work you will do. On this page you will write the subjects that you wish information about from the psychic storehouse of Cosmic Memory. If it is health, write it down, and the questions you wish to ask. If it is about how to make more money or going into a new business, write this down also, asking guidance. If it is some problem that you wish this psychic mind to solve, write that down also. It is important that your mind work in a neat and orderly fashion, for the Cosmic Memory of the universe obeys laws of order and balance.

3. Now practice developing your powers of visual and auditory perception. Go back to the earliest days you can remember and recall the most dramatic and outstanding incidents in your life. When you start this process of psychic retrogression, you will be using your conscious and unconscious memory. It will amaze you at how many details your mind will pick up which you had forgotten for many years. As Cosmic Memory works in a kind of replay of past events, you will be duplicating the process with your own mind in this practice session. All of a sudden you may find a stream of consciousness flowing into your own mind from a mysterious source, and then you will realize you are receiving psychic impulses from the Cosmic Memory which you had never thought possible. When this cosmic overflow begins, *let it continue* to pour its stream

of ideas, suggestions and instructions through your conscious mind.

4. Consciously call up memory patterns of the people who were in your life in the early years who might now be gone out of this life. See their faces, hear their voices, live through some pleasant experience you shared together. Suddenly you may experience a psychic overtone from their minds; information that is valuable may come through to you.

How a psychic dream led to finding a hidden fortune

An example of this came to my personal attention. A young woman of twenty-five had lost her father and had been left penniless. She had never gone to work, for after her mother had died some years before, she had kept house for her father. Now with her father dead, she had no money and no way of getting any. She had studied psychic phenomena with me and knew how to go into psychic reverie and contact cosmic thought forces. This particular day she was sitting in her room, in a state of psychic reverie. She recalled her father as he was in life; his face, his voice, his smile and expression, all were vividly recalled. Then suddenly her father seemed to be in the room beside her, and his voice was in her ears, just as she had heard it in life. He said, "Go to the chest of drawers stored in the basement. In the back of one drawer you will find a secret compartment. Look inside that compartment." With that, her father's voice faded and she came out of her reverie, feeling a little foolish at the seeming improbability of really having heard her father speak. She thought that perhaps she had drifted off into a light sleep and dreamed the incident.

However, the dream was so vivid that she went to the basement and sought out the chest of drawers, and inspected each of the six compartments in the chest. On the back of the upper drawer, there was a false compartment which she opened and there she found a roll of big bills that totaled five thousand dollars!

5. Project yourself into the dimension of the future,

and ask the Cosmic Memory bank to give you clairvoyant pictures of what you will be doing a year, five years, ten years from now, *As there is no past, present or future in cosmic time,* but only one continuous form or flow of consciousness, which man breaks up into minutes, hours, months and years, this Cosmic Memory can project future events as well as review past events.

See yourself financially well-off and travelling to places you mentally select. The gift of prophecy is often born in such moments of Cosmic recall of *future events.* The psychic thought is parent to the act, and in these psychic sessions you may actually be previewing some of the things you will do in the future.

HOW PSYCHIC PROJECTION WORKED
A FINANCIAL WINDFALL

I know of one incident where this type of psychic projection into the dimension of the future, worked for a lady who had studied these laws of psychic phenomena in our classes in New York.

When the ship *The France,* came to New York on its first trip, this lady cut a picture of it out of the papers, and put it into her scrapbook of destiny. She sat in psychic reverie daily and projected herself into the future, visualizing herself on the ship, eating in the sumptuous dining room, dancing in the night club, sunning herself in a deck chair on its spacious decks. At another time, when the ship was docked in New York, she went aboard to see it in person. She walked through the entire ship; she saw the cabins where she had projected herself. She came away with the feeling that one day, somehow, she would be sailing to France on the ship. At the time she did not have the money for such a trip and seemingly there was no way of getting it.

Three months after she began this process of psychic projection into the future, a letter arrived from an Aunt who lived in Ohio, whom she had not seen in years. Enclosed was a check for one thousand dollars! With it was an explanation that she wanted her to use the money to go on a long vacation.

Many times such psychic impressions will come through in dreams and they will be prophetic of an event that is to occur to a certain person at a definite time.

A DREAM OF AN EVENT OF DANGER

Mrs. Anna J. had such a psychic dream. She dreamed that her brother, who lived in Australia was swimming in the ocean. She suddenly saw him going down and crying for help. She awakened from the dream and told her husband how troubled she was. He assured her it was only a dream and had no reality to it, but she still felt vaguely disturbed. A few days later a letter arrived from her brother telling how he had nearly drowned in a riptide which had pulled him under and how he had cried out for help. A lifeguard had saved him, but it was a close call. How could the cosmic mind of the universe have recorded this event *which had not yet occurred?* It is possible that events are frozen in time and space, and are known to the Cosmic Mind which created the universe and all therein.

YOU POSSESS A PSYCHIC TIME CLOCK WITHIN YOU

There is a psychic and biological time clock within your own mind and body. At a certain age your body stops growing; at certain periods of life, the reproductive functions begin; we marry, have families, and mature, under the impetus of some higher cosmic and psychic force and intelligence. We can set this psychic time clock to control events in our future and make them happen on schedule.

By projecting these psychic impulses in definite pictures, words, or instructions to the higher psychic brain centers, we can trigger the psychic mechanism in our minds which regulates the happenings in the dimension we know as time. In the realm of mind and spirit there is no past, present or future; there is only the eternal now, and it is in this dimension of timelessness that the Cosmic Memory works to perform its miracles of creativity.

Summary of Chapter 4

1. How to tap the Cosmic Memory bank and use it for building your future.
2. The way this Cosmic Memory works throughout nature to create all living things.
3. The miracles of creativity that this Cosmic Mind performs.
4. How to use this psychic storehouse for finding your right work, creating happiness, romantic fulfillment, and achieving success and true serenity.
5. The gift of psychic prophecy which may be tapped by the higher mind and used for predicting future events.
6. Finding inspiration and creative guidance through the Cosmic Memory, the power that all geniuses used throughout history.
7. How to use Cosmic Memory to find lost articles, hidden treasures in the earth and sea, and build a fortune.
8. How to channelize cosmic magnetism to attract and influence important people in your life.
9. The dynamic steps to contact the psychic storehouse of Cosmic Memory for all purposes.
10. How one woman discovered five thousand dollars hidden in a chest of drawers, guided by the psychic voice of her father.
11. How to use cosmic and psychic memory to re-create the past and project the future.
12. How Cosmic Memory works through psychic dreams to predict the future and guide one to his destiny.
13. How a psychic dream predicted near-drowning thousands of miles away.

66

14. How to set the psychic and biological clock within your own psychic centers and project definite pictures, words, and instructions which will regulate happenings in your future.

chapter 5

Psychic Precognition—
the Key to Mold and Develop
Your Destiny

Psychic precognition means to know happenings in the future.

Can you actually know what events will take place in your future?

Does man have some kind of inner psychic knowledge which can show him how to mold and shape his destiny?

This power works in nature perfectly; the caterpillar *knows* it is to become a butterfly and weaves its cocoon to prepare for that momentous event.

A baby's body cells *know* they will mature and become a fully developed person and nature makes provision for the bones to grow and the cells to multiply until that future growth is achieved.

You possess psychic precognition naturally, and you may tap this power and use it to guide your entire life in the future.

YOU MAY ALREADY BE MORE PSYCHIC THAN YOU THOUGHT POSSIBLE

Have you ever felt that a certain event was going to occur and then have it happen exactly as you felt it would? Perhaps it was some trivial thing, like knowing you were going to run into a close friend or relative on the street on a certain day, or hearing from someone by mail that you have been seriously thinking about. Or you may have felt psychically that a famous person in the news was going to be killed, or that an airplane was going to crash.

When these future events occur, you are experiencing what is known as *psychic precognition*—an awareness of a future event which has not yet occurred but which is destined to happen.

Can man really know the future?

Can you truly shape and mold the events of your life to fit into a predetermined pattern through the gift of psychic precognition or clairvoyance?

There is a great deal of scientific evidence by leading academic researchers in psychical phenomena, to prove that man may indeed know, to a great extent, the events of his future.

Where psychic precognition is found

This gift of psychic precognition is inborn in all living things. The psychic intuition implanted in all creation by some vast Cosmic Intelligence, assures all living, evolving forms of life that they shall assume certain shapes and perform certain functions and fulfill themselves perfectly, according to some great cosmic blueprint.

There are two aspects to psychic precognition: One is CLAIRVOYANCE, the ability to see any event that occurs in the future, or that has occurred in the past. The other aspect is CLAIRAUDIENCE, the ability to hear the psychic voice, either within the ear, as an actual voice, or through the medium of words that come as ideas.

The ability to know the future, through clairvoyance or clairaudience, is known as psychic precognition.

HOW PSYCHIC WARNINGS CAME TO THESE FAMOUS MEN

Lincoln had a clairvoyant dream of his own death a few days before it happened and told members of his household of it. If he had followed this psychic warning he might have been spared from death.

John F. Kennedy accurately had a clairvoyant vision that he might be assassinated.

Dr. Martin Luther King, in a stirring speech a short

time before he was murdered, told of his premonition that he might not live much longer.

There is no doubt that these psychic warnings came from the higher, Cosmic Intelligence which we all may tap, and that these illustrious men could have avoided their tragic fate. But, it may be argued, if the event was predestined by some vast cosmic force, *how could they have avoided it?* The answer to this is that all our lives have a psychic format. The sequence of events is inevitable and known to the psychic timetable of the cosmos, but the individual events making up that sequential flow of events *can be altered, averted or deliberately courted,* by the conscious will that *selects* the daily events of our lives. This psychic censor is more acute in some than in others; you can decide to be reckless and drive your car at a hundred miles an hour while intoxicated; if you meet death through this irresponsible act, shall it be claimed that it was in your psychic and cosmic timetable and that you could not have averted this tragic fate? Rather, was it not due to the faulty mechanism of your psychic censor which did not inhibit you in this reckless act?

Many times we are saved from disaster by listening to this inner psychic voice, and we avoid the dangerous act that might have resulted in injury or death. These instances are often unrecorded by psychic researchers, for they are seldom reported, but the more dramatic instances where a tragedy occurs and the recipient of the psychic message did *not* obey his psychic impulse, are reported by relatives or friends, and enter the records of psychical researchers.

AN INSTANCE OF PSYCHIC PRECOGNITION THAT COULD HAVE PROTECTED A PERSON

An instance that was reported to me by a member of my lecture group was that of a woman, Mrs. W., who was baking bread one day, when she felt a sensation of burning in her right hand. She had not burned herself, but at the same moment she felt the pain, she saw a mental flash of a car burning.

Mrs. W. rushed to the phone and called her daughter,

who went to college in a distant city, and told her of the psychic warning she had received; she begged her daughter to be careful in driving her car. The girl thought her mother was being overemotional and fearful and laughed at the warning.

That afternoon, this girl was driving her car home from school; the motor caught fire; she tried to beat out the flames and her right hand was severely burned!

If this girl had listened to the psychic warning of her mother, it is likely that she could have averted the disaster. She might at least have had a fire extinguisher in her car. The fact that she had no faith in her mother's clairvoyant vision paved the way to her injury.

HOW PSYHIC PRECOGNITION SAVED A GIRL FROM DEATH

Another instance, which was reported to me by a famous movie star in Hollywood, was that which occurred in a well-known studio. She was sitting on a set, preparing to go on in a scene. A huge crystal chandelier was suspended on a cable above her head. Suddenly, without any apparent reason, she received a psychic warning: get out from under that chandelier! She said she had not even considered the danger, but on that psychic impulse she got up immediately, moved to another location, and as she did so the huge chandelier fell on the exact spot where she had been sitting! It would have killed or badly injured her, if she had not moved.

We all receive these psychic messages throughout our lives; some of us listen to them and live to tell about it; others ignore these warnings and are injured or killed because of failure to recognize the reality of psychic precognition which *knows the future and can tell us what to do to avert disaster*.

THE ART OF PSYCHIC CASTLE-BUILDING

You can project your psychic visions to the future and actually influence the events that you want to occur. This method I have named PSYCHIC CASTLE-BUILDING. Psychic precognition is used in this method, but instead of trying to see what future events will make up your destiny, you actually project the psychic and clairvoyant images into the dimension of the future that you want to shape your destiny.

How to use psychic castle-building

1. Sit quietly in a room and let your mind wander effortlessly in what we call daydreaming .
2. Visualize the work you want to do in the future; project yourself into the fourth dimensional realm of psychic reality and see yourself in your own business, writing books, acting, composing songs, inventing objects, investing in the stock market—anything that you want your higher psychic senses to make a reality of.
3. Visualize yourself actually doing the things that you project into the future. As you build these mental and psychic castles in the air, you are tapping the fourth dimensional realm of mind and spirit, and you release a spiritual form of creative protoplasm which will begin to create the actual reality which you have psychically projected into your future.
4. As you sit in the mystic silence, ask the higher psychic mind within for instructions as to how to solve your problems; how to make more money; how to win and hold love; how to buy that home or that car that you desire; then sit quietly and let your mind be in a serenely relaxed state, as you wait for the responses from your higher psychic brain centers. The answers may come in your hearing words, in flashes of ideas, through imaginative pictures, or in feelings that you have to do certain things.
5. After receiving your instructions and answers, set them into motion in the outer objective realm. Remember that psychic impulses come to you in the inner, subjective realm of passive, psychic and creative energy. You must do something about the psychic impulses you receive and

72

carry out some plan of action that is given to you in your psychic reverie. The more you use these psychic impulses, the stronger they will come to you.

THE PSYCHIC KALEIDOSCOPE
OF INNER SOUL POWER

Man possesses within himself a vast psychic kaleidoscope of inner soul power, which he can tap to create new objects, new situations and new combinations that make up a brilliant and colorful destiny.

You have seen a kaleidoscope, which children play with. It is an elongated tube, with bits of colored glass at one end; when the instrument is turned in different directions, the colored particles of glass fall into amazing new patterns of brilliant colors; no two are ever alike.

The inner soul power that man may tap with higher psychic vision to predict and shape his future is similar in function. As you hold various psychic pictures in your consciousness, and turn to this psychic source of energy and power within your own soul, you will receive direct messages, thought forms and pictures and projections of ideas that you can use to shape a brilliant and happy destiny.

EIGHT STEPS TO TAKE FOR USING
PSYCHIC PRECOGNITION TO MOLD
AND DEVELOP YOUR FUTURE

The following dynamic steps done with patient expectation will yield great psychic and concrete benefits for you.

1. Sit in the psychic silence EACH day and become a receiving station for psychic impressions, thought forms and messages. Try to make your conscious mind a blank, and then hold in your consciousness one thought or idea that you wish information about. It may be some practical information such as: What should I do to make my business a greater success? Or you may want to know some future event such as: Where should I live for my greatest

73

happiness and good? You may want to receive some inspiration for a creative work: How can I best develop my talents as an artist? (A singer, actor, dancer, designer, beautician, or any other creative or artistic person may do the same.)

After you have held the thought in the forefront of your mind for a short period of time, relax completely and keep your eyes closed, awaiting psychic thought forms, information and instruction. Sometimes these ideas will come through your own imagination, for the psychic powers work through your own mental apparatus. Let these imaginative pictures pass through the forefront of your consciousness, and project yourself into them as if they are real, living scenes which you experience.

2. To help the psychic processes, you can exercise the function of your imagination by deliberately passing a series of scenes through your mind's eye. See yourself on a ship bound for Hawaii or Europe or Africa. Experience the sensation of really being there. Or project yourself into the dimension of the future by seeing yourself in your own business, or living in the home you choose, or being married to the person you desire. There is a very close connecting link between the psychic brain centers and your imagination, and what you conceive you may achieve. Always man's dreams preceded his actions, and you will stir the psychic nerve centers into positive forms of creative action by this exercise of your imaginative faculties.

3. Use the psychic gift of clairvoyance and clairaudience to project scenes of the future and to hear the psychic voice within telling you of future events that will occur in your life. This form of psychic vision must be deliberately encouraged and courted, for the psychic brain centers have been unused for so many years, in the average person's case, that he must stimulate these centers consciously.

Write down a list of things you wish to receive information about in your own future life. These can be anything that interests you. Here is a sample list that you might use, or you can make up one of your own:

What type of work am I best suited to?
Where should I build my future life?

Whom should I marry?

How can I attract my future mate?

How can I make more money to pay my debts and give me the things I desire?

What steps can I take to solve my problems?

How can I achieve a more dynamic personality?

How can I overcome the negative emotions of fear, worry, self-consciousness and inferiority?

What can I do to overcome this bad habit of smoking (drinking, gambling, or laziness)?

How can I develop my creative gifts and talent and find the right outlet for them?

4. As you sit in psychic reverie and practice this art of psychic precognition, look at some object that has already been invented and ask this higher psychic mind how you can change it or invent something even better. Then sit quietly and let this higher psychic mind give you answers to your questions. Most of our great inventions have come about because of this reflective psychic mind power.

How an inventor used psychic precognition to become wealthy

A man I once met in Honolulu at my lectures, told me how he had been guided by this psychic power to the invention of the mercury electric switch for the home which works noiselessly. He asked his psychic higher mind how he could perfect a switch which would not awaken people when it was turned on or off at night. One day in his psychic contemplation the idea came through in a flash. This one idea made this man millions of dollars.

5. Create *psychic cosmographs* of the things you want to attract and project them to the Cosmic Mind which creates all things, in your daily psychic practice sessions. Cut pictures out of magazines and newspapers of the objects you want to magnetize and attract. Form a psychic scrapbook of destiny, in which you paste these pictures. It can be a new car, a beautiful home, a fur coat,

a pearl necklace, a refrigerator, air-conditioner, vacuum cleaner, furnishings for your home, or a trip to some foreign country. Put these cosmographs in the book, and then concentrate each day for a few minutes on each picture, projecting it into the dimension of reality by seeing yourself driving the car, living in the home, wearing the fur coat, taking the trip to Europe. As you concentrate on each psychic cosmograph, feel the emotion you would experience if you actually had the real thing that you desire.

HOW A WOMAN ATTRACTED A
$5,000 MINK COAT FOR HERSELF

One woman in my lecture group in New York City, had heard me tell in class how to use these cosmographs to project the psychic picture of what one desired, and she began to project the cosmograph of a beautiful mink coat. She worked as a maid in a rich home, and her salary was inadequate for her to ever dream of buying such an expensive coat. However she had faith that through psychic means the coat would come to her.

One day, a wealthy woman sitting behind her in the class on psychic development, saw this woman's thin, shabby cloth coat. It was a cold winter night, and she was stirred into action. She was buying a new mink coat, and she wrapped her old coat, which was in excellent condition, into a gift box, and brought it to class the next week and gave it to the woman who had been projecting the cosmograph of the fur coat! Neither of these women had spoken aloud about their desires to give or to receive a mink coat, but the Cosmic Mind had received the cosmograph from one mind and projected it to the other mind, through psychic precognition.

6. Look about you in your own environment and ask the higher psychic mind: Give me guidance as to how I can improve my life and change it for the better. Then sit in the silence and wait for ideas to come through. If nothing comes through at a practice session, do not lose faith or give up. Many times these psychic impressions

will work best when you are busy doing something else, and then they just pop into your mind from out of nowhere *once you have taken adequate psychic steps.*

7. Select some outstanding person you wish to contact psychically and who may be able to help you achieve your goal in life. You can psychically project your thought forms and instructions to another person's mind, and cause him to be magnetized into helping you achieve your objective. This is a form of psychic hypnosis, and we have discussed it more thoroughly in another section of this book. You are using natural laws, and are not violating any moral or spiritual principles as long as your psychic projections are for your own good and not harmful to any other person.

Hold the person's face in mind during your psychic practice sessions. Call the person by name, talk in a soft, gentle voice, exactly as if he were in the room. Structure your request in positive words and phrases. *Example:* John, I want your help. You are in a position to make my dreams come true. I want you to get that better job for me. You will hear my psychic request and grant me my wish. I will work intelligently and hard, and be a credit to you. I know I am capable, and you will recognize my talent and advance my interests in this job.

8. You have the power to select the psychic patterns you wish to project into your future through precognition. To do this you must use the gift of clairvoyance; that is, see with your inner vision *the actual situation, object, person or event that you want to manifest in your future destiny.*

Precognition, used in this sense, means to actually recognize the event you wish to project into your future, before it actually occurs.

How a woman selected her husband psychically

An example of how this works is that of a woman I knew who chose mentally the image of the man she wished to marry. She did not know him, but she projected in her daily psychic practice sessions the image of a man with a

77

certain build, features, and character. She visualized him going to dances with her, taking her to movies, to dinner, proposing marriage; she saw the actual wedding in the church, with her relatives all present. She projected the home they would have in the country; the business he would be in. She kept at this psychic practice for three months. One night she went to a local club with a man she knew, but whom she did not love, and there she was introduced to the very man she had psychically been projecting! There was an instant wave of recognition and magnetic attraction between them. As they danced together he said, "I feel as if I've known you all my life."

Two months later this man proposed marriage to her. She married him, and the church wedding and all the details she had psychically projected came to pass, including the honeymoon in Hawaii, as she had seen it in her psychic precognition.

This type of psychic precognition helps shape the events you choose for your future life pattern and destiny in their tiniest detail.

Almost all careers are built upon this form of psychic precognition. People often use this higher power subconsciously, not consciously realizing they are tapping a vein of higher psychic intelligence within their minds which automatically projects the future they have selected.

Summary of Chapter 5

1. How you can use the gift of psychic precognition which is born in everyone and may be developed.
2. How psychic precognition works in nature to regulate the universe and all cosmic activity.
3. How to develop clairvoyance and clairaudience so you may see future events and hear the inner voice of psychic guidance.
4. How Lincoln, Kennedy and Martin Luther King had psychic advance warning of their assassinations.

5. How to use the power of choice and will to shape your future.
6. Psychic vision warning a girl of danger through fire.
7. How a famous actress was saved from death through precognition.
8. How to use psychic castle-building to mold events of your future.
9. The psychic kaleidoscope of inner soul power and how to project new combinations of events for your future.
10. Eight steps you can take to increase the power of psychic precognition.
11. How one woman used this power of precognition to attract a five thousand dollar mink coat for herself at no cost.
12. How psychic precognition helped a woman to marry the man of her choice.

chapter 6

How to Avoid Danger
and Achieve Personal Safety
Through Psychic Guidance

A wave of fear is sweeping through the country today; fear engendered by danger to our personal welfare and safety. There is an atmosphere of hatred, ill-will and hostility, street rioting, assaults against the person, armed robbery, and murder, all of which show no signs of lessening.

The latest releases by the F.B.I. and local police show a shocking rise in crimes of personal violence, rape, robbery and murder. Forces of anarchy of all types are rampant in this country today which threaten law and order.

Although living in this atmosphere of danger, violence and fear, you can definitely do something to enlist the aid of your higher psychic guidance to build an invisible mental and psychic defense against the forces of terror and violence.

Fear generates a psychic paralysis which dulls the intuitive faculties of your higher mind. We are told in the Bible, "That which ye fear shall be visited upon you." *You will attract what you put into your consciousness.* If you insulate yourself against fear and build your psychic defense mechanism with a positive program of mental preparation, you can avoid danger and achieve personal safety from threats of violence and assault, even though it may occur all around you.

HOW A WOMAN WAS SAVED FROM ATTACK

A woman who had attended many of my lectures, was getting into her car late one night on a dark street, when a young man crowded into the front seat beside her. In his upraised hand was a hammer. He muttered, "If you scream I'll kill you!"

The woman had learned in a study of psychic phenomena and metaphysics that in such a situation she must instantly insulate herself against fear by making a statement of truth. She affirmed to herself, "I am in the magic circle of God's protective light and nothing can hurt me." Then some higher power of intuition prompted her to say aloud, "If you want my money, you can take it. I know how terrible your mother would feel if you did anything to make her ashamed of you."

Why she said this, she never knew, but something prompted her to say it in a clear, fearless voice. The young man's arm dropped to his side, as if paralyzed, and he burst into tears. He said, "I don't know what made me do this. I'm on dope and I needed money to get a fix. What you said about my mother made me terribly ashamed of myself." Without another word he opened the car door and vanished into the night.

This woman reported to me that if she had not known how to contact her higher psychic centers in that emergency she might have been badly injured, if not killed.

SELF-PRESERVATION IS AN INSTINCT OF THE HIGHER PSYCHIC MIND

The self-preservation instinct is one of the functions of your higher, psychic mind. When the danger threatens, this higher mind knows intuitively what to do. The scent of fear will cause a dog to instinctively protect itself by attacking the object it fears. Ferocious animals, like lions or tigers, will not attack a child who has not yet learned to fear.

In planning your psychic campaign to protect yourself in times of danger and achieve personal safety, be aware of these facts about danger:

Most dangerous situations can be avoided, if your intuition guides you, for it will automatically alert you, like a psychic alarm bell that rings in your higher mind centers.

You can sensitize your psychic centers to a high degree

of alertness by building the psychic sensors which tell you when to expect trouble, how to avoid it, when you should flee, or resist.

You will have an unusual degree of psychic awareness about people, which will intuitively tell you when they are thinking of robbery, attack or other crimes of personal violence.

HOW A WOMAN FOILED ROBBERS
THROUGH PSYCHIC GUIDANCE

An example of how one woman foiled a hold-up in a hotel, proves this point of psychic protection against danger. She was a cashier at the desk, and she observed two young men come in and ask at the desk where the public telephone was. She felt a vague sense of unrest about them, and she watched them as they walked across the lobby to the telephone booths. She had a strong psychic hunch that these men were up to something. Nothing in their appearance gave them away; they were both well-dressed, even polite in their actions. However, she put in a call to the police saying she suspected two men of being criminals and asked for help.

When the men returned from the phone booth they stopped at the desk and one engaged the clerk in conversation about a room, while the other strolled over to the cashier's window and quietly took out a revolver and demanded the money. The woman did not oppose him, but gave him the receipts, praying that help would come. Just as the two men started towards the door, two policemen entered, and the cashier screamed out that she had been robbed. The officers were on the alert, drew their revolvers, and without firing a shot, the two hoodlums put up their hands and were soon safely in handcuffs. Luckily the radio patrol car had been cruising nearby and responded immediately to this woman's call for help.

You will be guided intuitively to the avoidance of danger areas in your life, if you learn how to stimulate your psychic sensors, so they will alert you when your life is in danger. This can cause you to avoid districts where crime is rampant; dark streets, short-cuts through alleys or unoccupied city lots or other areas where criminals lurk. You will know when it is safe to be in certain areas, or when you should escape danger by being aware that something is about to happen.

YOUNG MAN IGNORED PSYCHIC SENSORS AND WAS SHOT

A young man who had this type of accident because he ignored the psychic sensors which would have guided him to safety, happened to be in a bar when two robbers came in with drawn guns. They took the money from the bartender, and then began to rob the customers. This young man had a hundred and fifty dollars and personal jewelry. When he was asked for his money he resisted the robbers and was shot in the abdomen. He lived, but was in the hospital for weeks, and the trouble and pain were not worth the money he would have saved if he had been successful in resisting the robbers.

His intuitive instinct should have saved him, for the urge to live is the strongest instinct in the human consciousness. He would probably have been unharmed if he had followed this instinct, as the others in the bar did.

THE SEVEN THREATS TO LIFE AND SAFETY

There are seven main areas of threats to your personal safety. These should be understood, so when you are confronted with danger in any of these categories, you will have had a kind of psychic preview of what you should do and how to act in the emergency.

1. Danger through fire
2. Threats of drowning
3. Accidents through motor vehicles
4. Accidents involving airplanes, machinery, etc.
5. Personal assaults, attacks by rapists or robbers

83

6. Armed robbery with knives, guns or other weapons
7. Accidents through natural catastrophes such as floods, hurricanes and cyclones, lightning, etc.

PSYCHIC REGIME TO AVERT DANGER FROM ANY OF THESE SEVEN SOURCES

1. Have faith in your higher psychic centers being able to guide and protect you. You can insulate yourself from danger by mentally building a wall around you, which I call the protective magic circle of Cosmic Mind. By affirming each day, when you set out in the morning for your day's activities, "I am in the center of my cosmic magic circle of protective power, and nothing can harm me," you will stimulate your psychic centers to unusual degrees of awareness and sensitivity. You will feel a sense of serenity and calmness which will cause you to act instinctively in the right way if any danger should threaten you.

2. Remove all fear of danger from your mind; remember fear paralyzes the psychic sensors which could warn you of threats against your safety, and also tell you how to act in the presence of danger. To keep yourself from fear, carry with you a small card in your purse or wallet which you can conveniently see several times a day, the twenty-third Psalm which begins, "The Lord is my Shepherd, I shall not want. . . ." Firmly believe this spiritual truth, and you will feel its radiatory power of courage and protection throughout your everyday activities. When confronted with dangerous situations repeat the first line of this statement, and you will feel its protective psychic power.

A BANK ROBBER FOILED BY GIRL'S COOL HEAD

A girl who used this psychic method for protection, was a cashier in a bank in New York City. She had prepared her psychic sensors for any emergency that might arise, well knowing that one day she might be confronted with an emergency.

One day a young man appeared at her window and handed her a note and a brown paper bag. The note said, "I am desperate, put the money in the bag and give it to me, and no one will be hurt. I have enough TNT here to blow up this bank." The girl had been told if such a situation arose, she should quietly hand over the money and not raise an alarm, for it might endanger her life. However, some psychic response of her higher mind told her this man was bluffing. She acted on her psychic hunch and screamed for one of the guards. The young man started to run from the bank, but he was caught by two guards. He was unarmed and had no TNT on him. The girl's psychic guidance proved correct because she had prepared herself psychically for this possibility of danger.

3. When confronted with situations of danger through fire or threats of drowning, do not panic, for remember— your psychic forces are then paralyzed and made inoperable when you panic and give in to fear. If you have prepared yourself by a kind of psychic preview of danger by asking your higher psychic center, *What would I do if . . . ?* then, in your mind's eye you received a psychic preview of dangerous situations which might conceivably confront you. *You will automatically be alerted* as to how to avoid these dangerous situations, or if they do occur, what you should do to protect yourself with psychic instinct.

HOW PSYCHIC PREVIEW OF A FIRE WORKED FOR ONE WOMAN

One woman I know had a psychic premonition of danger through fire. Her husband was a travelling salesman, and stayed in hotels throughout the country. This woman, in doing psychic protective work, had a dream one night in which she saw her husband trapped in his hotel room by a fire. She awakened with a sense of deep fear. She went back to sleep, and the dream returned. Now, thoroughly alarmed, she called the hotel where she knew her husband was staying in a distant city and awakened him from a sound sleep. "I had a terrifying dream of a fire!" she exclaimed. "Are you all right?"

Her husband replied, "Of course I'm all right. It was just a bad dream—go back to sleep and forget it."

But in the days ahead, the woman could not forget the vividness of her dream of danger through the fire. When her husband came home, she was insistent that he do something to protect himself in the event of a fire in a hotel on future trips. She begged him to carry a long, knotted piece of rope, with a steel hook on it, so if there were a fire and he found himself trapped, he could escape by his window even if there were no fire escape.

He finally acceded to her insistent demands that he protect himself from the danger of fire. In his suitcase was a strong piece of rope, with a hook on its end to be fastened to some object or the windowsill, in the event of fire.

Several weeks passed and the woman did not have her dream again, but one night, at three A.M. her phone rang. It was her husband calling from a distant city. He said, "You were so right about that fire! A fire broke out on my floor tonight, and when I opened the door of my room the hall was so full of smoke I would surely have suffocated. I had a room on the second floor, and in a matter of moments, I had my rope ladder hanging out of the window and climbed down to safety." Fortunately, no one was killed in that fire, but how often have people been killed because they had no warning of such a disaster.

4. When you are confronted with danger, instantly ask your higher psychic mind for guidance. Try to avoid becoming tense through fear; relax if possible and realize that your intuition, psychically developed will give you the correct instructions for saving yourself.

How a girl saved herself from a riptide because of psychic training

A girl who had come to my lectures in California, used this psychic secret to save her life. She was swimming at

Santa Monica beach, and she was caught in a riptide that started pulling her far from shore. Her first moment of panic made her want to struggle, and she would surely have become exhausted, and drowned, but suddenly her psychic center recalled one sentence from a lecture I had given: "Let go and let God . . . ." She instantly had an urge to stop struggling; *she let the riptide take her out* a quarter of a mile or so, while she calmly saved her strength and kept her head above water. Then, when the tide had spent its force, she slowly swam back to shore and safety.

5. Practice the art of clairvoyant pre-vision, in which you consciously review events that might occur in the future where you need psychic guidance and protection for the safety of your life.

Go into silence for this practice session, and ask your higher mind questions to which you will receive psychic answers:

What would I do if suddenly confronted with fire?
How should I act if a robber with a gun or knife stops me?
How should I handle myself if I am caught up in a street riot?
What should I do if attacked by a rapist?
How can I avoid danger in water?
What can I do to avoid danger through accidents?
If assaulted by a mugger what action should I take?

As you pass each of these hypothetical problems through the psychic fabric of your consciousness, you will receive suitable impulses or responses, which you will store in your memory bank, to be utilized if and when you require them.

6. Follow that psychic and clairvoyant hunch when it comes, for it may save your life. How often are people warned not to take a certain airplane, or ship, or get into a certain car or bus. They ignore these subtle psychic warnings, or feel that they are foolish, and they are often involved in tragic accidents.

An instance in my own life where I received such a psychic hunch and followed it, saved me from what might have been a real disaster. I was in Athens, Greece, and

87

wanted to return to New York by ship, but there was no ship leaving Piraeus, that went directly to America. I was advised by the travel agent to take a boat from Piraeus to Naples, where a new luxury liner was about to make its maiden voyage. I obtained a ticket for this trip, which was to take place in a few days, and then feelings of unease began to assault me. I had never feared fire on ships, for I had crossed the oceans many times in perfect safety, but a persistent kind of psychic warning flashed through my mind to cancel my trip and take another ship from Piraeus, direct to New York at a later date.

I obeyed my psychic warning and cancelled the ticket. A few days later, while still in Greece, I listened to a radio newscast which said that the other ship had caught fire while several hundred miles out to sea and had to return to Naples!

How many times these warnings flash into your mind from your higher psychic centers, and you may think that this is your timid conscious mind appraising a situation, but actually it is your psychic intuitive mind giving you the warning to preserve your life. This function works so closely in cooperation with the conscious mind that many people laugh off these warnings as being silly and go on to do the dangerous act that may threaten life and limb. Your entering into psychic communication as pointed out in this book will never lead to any doubt as to true psychic communication being received.

7. Follow your psychic hunches and take all reasonable precautions to avert disaster, but if you should suddenly be confronted with a natural catastrophe, such as an earthquake, cyclone, flood or rioting, do not feel that you have been deserted by your psychic guardian angel. You must invoke the law of self-preservation regardless, and instantly obey the alarm bell of your higher psychic mind which will tell you what to do in that emergency.

To fortify yourself against such natural calamities, write on a card this saying from the Bible which you should see as often as possible and memorize:

"A thousand shall fall on thy left and ten thousand shall fall on thy right, but it shall not come nigh thee.

Only with thine eyes shalt thou behold the reward of the wicked."

We cannot account for the mystery of misfortune, but if it should strike, know that you are psychically insulated from danger, and somehow, you will survive the various catastrophes that occur during every normal lifetime.

WOMAN WAS PSYCHICALLY WARNED OF SKIING ACCIDENT

A woman who had practiced these laws of psychic phenomena under my guidance was warned of a skiing accident to her husband through the higher communication. This woman and her husband were skiing enthusiasts, and had never been injured. There were no abnormal fears in either of their minds, but one night the woman dreamed that her husband was skiing down a slope when his ski hit a submerged object and he fell breaking his right leg in two places. The dream was so vivid that she awakened and noted the time. It was two in the morning. She told her husband about her dream and he laughed it off, and told her to go back to sleep.

The next weekend, as was their custom in the winter, they went skiing. The woman had been unable to persuade her husband not to go. Everything went fine during the period of time before lunch. Then shortly after lunch, they were moving over the same area where they had skied in the morning, when suddenly the man's skis hit a submerged object and he was catapulted through the air, falling heavily at a distance. He cried out with pain, and when help came, it was found that he had broken his right leg in two places, exactly as his wife had dreamed it the week before. As her husband was carried off to the hospital, she looked at her watch and it was exactly two o'clock! Here, the warning should have been followed by asking for definite guidance as to times to ski safely, and where.

Summary of Chapter 6

1. How to avoid the deadly paralysis of psychic centers brought on by indulging the emotion of fear in situations of personal danger.
2. How a woman was saved from attack by following psychic responses.
3. How to build the instinct of self-preservation through psychic guidance.
4. Psychic guidance caused a woman to foil a robber who threatened her safety.
5. How to stimulate your psychic sensors which will tell you of the approach of danger and what to do about it.
6. How a young man ignored these psychic sensors and was shot.
7. The seven danger areas in your life and how to avoid them through psychic guidance and intuition.
8. The psychic regime to avert danger in all departments of your life.
9. How to avoid panicking when danger confronts you, and turn to the higher psychic centers for instantaneous perfect guidance and safety.
10. How to use the art of psychic pre-vision, which will give you a preview of disaster areas in your life and show you how to psychically avoid their threat to your life and limb.
11. How the author was saved from shipboard fire through psychic vision and pre-knowledge of danger.
12. What to do if confronted with a natural catastrophe, such as earthquake, cyclone, flood or riot, and invoke the aid of your psychic guardian angel to protect you.

chapter 7

How to Use Psychic and Cosmic Improvisation to Become Successful and Rich

Fame, honor, riches and abundance can be showered upon you by the Cosmic Mind *when you learn how to use the laws of psychic and cosmic improvisation* which exist in all nature.

A maple tree does not create one single seed to assure the perpetuity of the species. Nature creates thousands— and then arms them with little parachutes which carry them on the wind, away from the shade of the mother tree, where they are more likely to find a place to grow and fulfill their destiny. This is cosmic improvisation.

You can use the same secret power to assure achieving your life destiny that nature uses in cosmic and psychic improvisation for all creation.

This higher psychic power can cause you to take the elements of your life and build a destiny of happiness and abundance, if you follow the cosmic blueprint that is engraved within your own immortal soul. From the building blocks of the universe, through cosmic improvisation, you can be guided to all the elements which make for successful living. You have the power to improvise from these cosmic building blocks a hovel, or a palace, *depending on how you use the psychic power you already possess.*

THE TEN FACETS OF THE UNIVERSAL DIAMOND OF SUCCESS

There are ten facets to the universal diamond of success, which your inner psychic guidance can bring into focus in your own life. You have been given the power to achieve the fulfillment of your destiny, and by knowing and applying the laws of cosmic improvisation you can attract and manifest all the priceless treasures that have been placed in the universe for you to enjoy.

1. A strong, healthy body with youth and vitality
2. Financial rewards and full remuneration for your life work
3. A useful social life and ego recognition
4. Romantic and marriage fulfillment, with a family of your own
5. Development of your creative gifts and talents
6. Cultural and intellectual achievements
7. The achievement of psychic and intuitive guidance
8. The overcoming of problems and mastery of fear, worry and other negative emotions
9. A dynamic and magnetic personality with the power to attract and hold friends
10. The achievement of spiritual balance: peace of mind and the soul's serenity

HOW TO USE PSYCHIC AND COSMIC IMPROVISATION

In the theater there is a branch of acting known as improvisation. The actor selects a certain role or scene, and then by a kind of intuitive function, he improvises the lines and the actions which he believes fit that character and make that scene come to life.

Similarly, there is a psychic and cosmic force in the universe which improvises and carries out dynamic action according to a predetermined pattern, to create whatever you select as your role in life. You can choose to become a villain or a romantic hero; a prince or a pauper; a slave or a king; a beggar or a rich man. You can make the lines of dialogue which you improvise sad or funny; romantic or crude; the people you choose for your supporting cast of characters in this universal drama may be high and lofty or shabby and lowly. You can make the setting one of drabness and ugliness or create and improvise, under psychic guidance, a magnificent tapestry of dreams, ideals and beauty with which to adorn yourself and your background. The choice is entirely up to you, and when you have once made this choice, psychic and cosmic improvisation will be invoked by your higher mind to carry out perfectly the destiny you have selected—the part which you wish to play in life.

This is exactly how you can harness the power of the psychic and Cosmic Intelligence in the universe, and improvise the events of your life, select the persons you wish to meet, choose the environment you desire, invent the situations you want, and infuse the elements of your life with the inspiration and vitality that will assure you of achieving a successful, full and abundant life. The higher psychic mind within you will work out the pattern you choose and help to flawlessly improvise the elements you need to create success and riches.

DO YOU KNOW WHAT YOU WANT IN LIFE?

Do you really know what you want in life? If you don't know whether you want this Cosmic Intelligence to create for you a pumpkin or an oak tree, how can your higher psychic mind guide you to your destiny? You must work with these cosmic laws, and the first place to begin is in *knowing what you want in life.*

YOUR AVAILABILITY OF PSYCHIC
AND COSMIC POWER

You can tap this psychic and cosmic power and utilize cosmic improvisation to become as rich as you wish to be, and to attract any portion of the abundance that is in the realm of nature.

There is no poverty in nature, it is only in man's consciousness. Psychic vision will show you how to tap the illimitable resources that are in the universe for you to use and enjoy. It is necessary for you to have FAITH in this power that can guide you to the hidden storehouse of riches in the universe.

HOW TO MOTIVATE YOUR PSYCHIC AND COSMIC IMPROVISATION

The following motivator program will effectively cultivate your full power of psychic and cosmic improvisation.

1. Sit in the silence and concentrate on the truth about the riches that are contained in the cosmic depository of treasures in the universe. Call this your *psychic inventory,* and list the material treasures of gold, silver, jewels and other things of value that exist. Then be aware of the natural treasures which you have been given in abundance: fruit grains, vegetables, milk and cheese and the multitude of other edible foods that have been created to nourish and sustain your life force. See how the oceans teem with food and other treasures, such as gold and oil, which scientists are now learning to tap. *Concentrate your psychic power on these treasures and ask the Cosmic Intelligence to guide you to find the abundance you desire.*

2. Now build the million dollar cosmic consciousness that will cause your higher psychic mind to improvise for you the actions which can produce all the riches you want. Adopt the mental attitude that you are already an heir to a kingdom, as the Bible says, and that you have inherited a universe. Put a psychic claim on that portion of the world's riches which you wish to have as your very own.

Make the psychic claim for money and material treasures upon the psychic and Cosmic Intelligence of the universe, and then wait for information to come through that will guide you to demonstrating the abundance you desire.

Psychic claim for money led this man to abundance

I once knew an artist who had three sons, and there seemed to be no way that he could sell his paintings and make enough to support his family comfortably. This man learned about the higher psychic power within his own

94

mind, and he knew that he was guided in his paintings to create beautiful landscapes which could be sold. But he did not know how to find a market for his works, so he asked this higher mind one day when he was in the silence, how he could go about selling his art works.

A psychic flash came through telling him: buy a small truck, load it with your paintings, park it beside the road where there is heavy traffic and be painting your scenes as people go by. At first thought, this seemed rather disappointing advice, for he could not imagine people buying his paintings from a truck parked beside the road. However, he had faith in the higher psychic mind and followed its instructions perfectly. He found a small, second hand panel truck, bought it, decorated its sides with his paintings and parked on a road leading from Hollywood to the beach areas. As he sat in a beret and smock painting by the side of the road, hundreds of motorists stopped to watch him. Soon they were buying his paintings, and from this small start this man soon bought a home in a fashionable valley, and educated his three sons, sending them to college.

Boldly make your psychic claim for happiness, peace of mind, social recognition, the making of friends, the building of a dynamic and magnetic personality. In fact, ask for all the ten facets of the universal diamond of success which are listed above, and the higher psychic mind within you will show you how to use the law of cosmic improvisation to achieve them.

3. Utilize the wealth and material possessions fully, which you are now using but which you do not actually own. Be aware of the treasures in the public libraries, the collected wisdom and knowledge from the greatest minds of the ages, which are yours for the asking. Enrich your own consciousness through studying the lives of these great geniuses, and stimulate the psychic centers of your brain by duplicating their thoughts and enriching your own intellect with their wisdom.

Go to your local art galleries and museums and make their historical masterpieces a part of your own consciousness. If you do not have the great paintings of the masters in your art gallery, buy reproductions of these paintings and study them, building your sense of values in art.

Study philosophy, psychology, astronomy, science, literature, music, physics, drama — all the creative impulses which the human mind has received from the Cosmic Mind of the universe, should be made a part of your sum total of consciousness. In this way you take on the cultural and intellectual lustre which the great geniuses of the past have given to the world, and they will become a part of your own cosmic improvisation, building a richer, fuller and more satisfying life for you.

4. Visit your public parks and buildings and claim these as part of your own heritage of riches and abundance. You will stimulate your higher psychic centers and be inspired to cosmic improvisation if you enrich your mind by feeling that you *now own and possess vast estates and public works which you may use and enjoy free of charge.* That public park is as much yours as any other person's. You need not have a staff of gardeners to take care of it. The public works, telephone company, gas and electric and water works, are *all yours to use and enjoy for a very small sum.* Think of the investment in terms of billions of dollars in these projects, in the highways, public transportation, taxis, buses, trolleys, subways and trains, which no millionaire could possibly afford—yet these great treasures are already yours to use and enjoy. By accepting these forms of abundance and supply here and now, you will help stimulate the psychic nerve centers of your own brain, which will guide you to improvise supply and abundance such as a steady income, security for the future, your own home, your own car, better clothing, education for your children and the hundreds of other little details which can make your life richer and more comfortable.

5. Be aware of the priceless treasures provided to you through your radio and television and motion pictures, which are yours for very little cost. No potentate of the Orient could have been able to afford a modern radio or television set, and yet, with a flip of a switch you can tune in a magnificent symphony or opera from the Metropolitan, or a million dollar movie, or a comedy program

that cost the producers hundreds of thousands of dollars. You can be royally entertained by the talents of a Jackie Gleason, a Lucille Ball or Milton Berle. You can command Greta Garbo to put on a special performance for you, or call upon the departed beings, such as John Barrymore, Tyrone Power, Clark Gable and Errol Flynn to entertain you with their great talents. When you doubt the power of your higher mind to enrich your life realize that *cosmic improvisation has already provided you with the greatest riches and treasures if you will but avail yourself of the bounties showered upon you.*

6. Sit in psychic meditation and hold the word *riches* in the forefront of your consciousness. Let your higher psychic centers improvise for you, in a kind of fantasy, the ideal life you would like to live. As thoughts are things, the mental and psychic energy you project in this type of fantasy daydreaming, has the power to attract to you the type of destiny you visualize and project. A thought is as real as a rainbow or a skyscraper, and your thoughts are the equivalents of material and physical things.

7. Make out a *psychic treasure map* to help guide your higher psychic sense in accumulating the treasures you desire.

Cut out the pictures of the house, the car and the things you desire and put them in your treasure map. Write down the type of work you wish to do in the future. Put down the gifts and talents you want to develop. Describe the ideal soul mate you wish to marry. Write out a list of stocks or other investments you wish to make to build your personal fortune and bring security. Write down the names of the foreign countries you wish to visit, the places you want to go for vacations, and then get travel literature from a travel agency, describing these places in detail.

One young man of twenty-three, who had always wanted to travel, but did not have the money to do so, used this psychic treasure map method for charting a trip to Africa. He was told by his higher psychic centers to apply for a job in the Peace Corps. He did so, and qualified, and soon found himself on his way to Africa, exactly as he had treasure-mapped it!

Another person I know who was guided by higher psychic power to round the world travel was a lady who worked as a beauty operator. She treasure-mapped two things she wanted her higher mind to improvise for her: A trip around the world, and a husband who was wealthy.

Her psychic senses guided her to a job on a round the world cruise ship, and on the ship she met a widower who was wealthy and who fell in love with and married her.

8. To stimulate your psychic brain centers and invoke the power of cosmic improvisation, study the lives of rich and successful persons and see how they have achieved wealth and fulfillment. Your psychic centers will release new and more stimulating information when you acquaint yourself with the facts about successful people and their accomplishments.

9. Daily attune your mind and psychic senses to the higher vibrations of the Cosmic Intelligence that rules the universe, so you will be better able to pick up the subtle vibrations which come through as psychic and intuitive guidance. Attune your mind to music and you will better understand music. Attune your mind to friendship, and you will better know how to make friends, and also be one. Attune your mind to love and you will be guided correctly to the right source for your fulfillment in love.

Your higher psychic mind must be tuned like a fine violin before you are able to receive the higher pulsations of psychic and intuitive guidance from the Cosmic Mind of the universe.

10. Use these *nine psychic motivators* to help inspire your higher psychic creative centers into dynamic action that will automatically tap the power of cosmic improvisation in your life:

1. Have a desire to do good with your money.
2. Strive to idealize your life and spiritualize your personality.
3. Have a love of creating beauty for others to enjoy.

4. Build your life dream on unselfish motivation, that includes the welfare of your family and the world.
5. Have a desire to bring about peace and brotherhood for the entire world.
6. Make it a point to daily express unselfish love for others.
7. Practice the art of forgiving others for their faults and injustices.
8. Strive to uplift, inspire, educate and beautify the world and make it a better place in which to live.
9. Share your happiness with other people.

Summary of Chapter 7

1. How you can duplicate the miraculous forces which create riches, through cosmic and psychic improvisation.
2. The ten facets of the universal diamond of success and how you may achieve them in your life.
3. How to choose the predetermined pattern of your destiny and invoke the universal law of psychic improvisation.
4. How to know what you want in your future life and how to use psychic and cosmic improvisation to have it.
5. The proof of universal riches and abundance and how you may tap an unending source of supply in your life.
6. The step by step regime for becoming rich and successful through psychic and cosmic improvisation.
7. How you can build the million dollar consciousness that will trigger the higher psychic centers of your brain and make you rich.
8. How one man put in a claim for riches and achieved financial independence and security.
9. How to channel the free universal riches through cosmic improvisation.

10. The psychic treasure map that will chart your future course to riches and abundance.
11. How to use the nine psychic motivators to inspire you to higher creative activity and dynamic action for building a fortune.

chapter 8

How to Focus Your Psychic
Powers Through the
Mirrorscope of Your Soul

What makes some men great and others mediocre?

Can anyone become a genius and create great works like a Shakespeare, Pasteur, Plato, Leonardo da Vinci or Edison?

Is there a psychic magic wand which you may wave that will automatically give you power to attract anything in life that you desire?

You can truly tap supernormal powers of the mind and soul and put yourself in tune with the soul of the universe, when you *learn how to focus your psychic powers through the mirrorscope of your soul*. You can become a genius and project a radiant stream of creative energy which can transform your life and circumstances.

THE COSMIC MIND THAT KNOWS
ALL LIFE'S SECRETS

There is a great Cosmic Intelligence in the universe which contains all the secrets of the past, present and future. It is here, in the mystical, invisible cosmic realm that man may tap the all-wise, all-powerful, all-knowing cosmic soul of the universe and focus its rays through his own higher mind in the mirrorscope of his soul. Then man takes on some of the omniscience, omnipotence and omnipresence which is a part of what Emerson called the over-soul of the universe.

Just as a mirror accurately reflects the image of what it sees, so too the mirrorscope of your soul has the ability to focus upon its supersensible surface the thought forms, images, emotions, ideas and creative powers which exist in the Cosmic Soul (which knows every event that has occurred in the past, everything that is happening in this present moment and everything that will ever happen in the future).

The psyche or soul in man is the spark of cosmic life which God has implanted in all His creation. It is now generally recognized by many scientists that some higher, Cosmic Intelligence does exist in the visible and invisible universe and that it is non-material in nature. Ths Cosmic Intelligence knows how to create everything that man needs for fulfilling his life destiny.

HOW TO LINK YOUR SOUL TO THE GOLDEN COSMIC CHAIN OF UNIVERSAL SOUL RADIATION

You can form a vast psychic network of soul power when you once learn how to link your soul to the golden cosmic chain of universal soul radiation. This network of psychic impulses will connect you with all past knowledge, and give you a psychic preview of the future, as well as reveal secrets that can cause you to live a healthy, happy and prosperous life in the immediate present.

Your psychic nerve centers are stimulated by exciting and stimulating thoughts. You can set up psychic impulses that radiate from your soul to the nerves of your brain and body, exactly reflecting through the mirrorscope of your soul, the total power, intelligence and life force and energy that is contained in the soul of the universe. This secret of pyramiding psychic power to absolute cosmic totality, can be utilized for many creative functions in your life. We shall now learn how to set up these psychic overtones of the soul and use them for constructive purposes in your life. This psychic escalation of dynamic spiritual energy is potent and can bring about miracle healing of the body, as well as many other demonstrations of physical and material benefits.

THE MASTER, JESUS, USED THIS COSMIC SECRET

This was undoubtedly the secret power that Jesus used when he performed his miracles of walking on water, changing water into wine, multiplying the loaves and fishes to feed the multitude, and causing the sick to be cured instantaneously. As His pure soul reflected the Cosmic Intelligence, He was enabled to form a spiritual link with the absolute cosmic totality of power and, through changing the molecular structure of matter by a psychic escalation of dynamic spiritual energy, He could create new forms of matter, revitalize the cells of sick bodies and regenerate them into the image of cosmic perfection.

There are certain spiritual keys which can form a cosmic link with man's soul and the soul of the universe. These six spiritual and psychic keys are:

1. Faith
2. Love
3. Good
4. Charity
5. Forgiveness
6. Prayer

When your soul is attuned to the highest spiritual and psychic forces in the universe, then the mirrorscope of your soul is better able to reflect the cosmic pulsations of universal intelligence and psychic guidance.

GREAT MEN WERE USUALLY GOOD MEN

The great men of history were usually good men, and had a deep love for humanity and a desire to give of their creative gifts for the good of the world. Seldom were these illumined souls selfish or concerned about earthly wealth or glory.

Some of these great souls of history who reflected

through the mirrorscope of their souls the golden light of good, love and truth were:

Moses, Buddha, Confucius, Christ—who revealed moral and spiritual codes which civilized and spiritualized mankind.

And in our own age we have had the examples of outstanding men and women, such as:

Lincoln, Churchill, George Washington Carver, Burbank, Edison, Pasteur, Mme. Curie, Florence Nightingale, Jane Addams, Joan of Arc, Helen Keller, and Father Damien, as well as thousands of other illumined souls too numerous to mention.

THE NEED FOR SOUL ATTUNEMENT

The mirrorscope of your soul can accurately reflect the Cosmic Intelligence of the soul of the universe *when it is accurately attuned to this higher power*.

Then it can know all secrets and have access to vast psychic and intuitive forces which can guide one to a great and glorious destiny.

I remember once when a concert pianist I knew was giving a concert in the ballroom of a famous hotel in New York City. On the raised platform was a magnificent, beautifully tuned Steinway concert grand piano. In an adjoining room, where the door stood ajar, was another concert grand piano, tuned to the same pitch as the one my friend was to play. The pianist sat down before the piano and struck a note on the keyboard. He said, "Now listen." I listened and heard a distant echo of the identical note he had just struck. It came from the piano in the other room! He remarked, "When two pianos are tuned alike, one sets up overtones which are echoed by the other."

This is exactly what happens when your soul is attuned to the psychic overtones of the soul of the universe. The above six keys can be used to give you this psychic attunement to the soul of the universe, and the wavelengths of knowledge, power, wisdom and guidance will be reflected in your soul.

We are told in the Bible, "God is Good," "God is Love." Therefore goodness and love form mystic, psychic chains that link us to the great cosmic soul of the universe.

We are also told in the Bible, "Thy faith hath made thee whole." Faith is another way by which we attune our soul's wavelength to that of the universe for psychic reception.

We are urged in the Bible to love our neighbor, to forgive seventy times seven, and this is the mystic formula for attuning the psychic reflector of your own immortal soul to the cosmic wavelengths on which the soul of the universe operates.

HOW TO FOCUS YOUR PSYCHIC POWERS THROUGH THE MIRRORSCOPE OF YOUR SOUL

1. For psychic escalation of dynamic spiritual energy, elevate your consciousness above the material realm when you go into psychic concentration and reverie. Repeat the Lord's Prayer or the twenty-third Psalm, or both, before you begin your psychic attunement to the soul of the universe.

2. Sit in the silence holding the mirrorscope of your mind and soul absolutely still. Do not reflect any worries, fears or earthly concern about problems in your life.

3. Now concentrate and reflect in the mirrorscope of your soul the cosmic quality of OMNISCIENCE—all-knowing, all-wise. Hold in the mirrorscope of your mind the word omniscience and say to yourself the following words, which will stimulate the higher, psychic centers of your mind.

"I now desire the cosmic quality of OMNISCIENCE. I ask for wisdom and knowledge, power to know the hidden secrets of the universe. I now elevate my consciousness above the realm of the physical and material universe and ascend into the spiritual realm of pure cosmic light and power. I am now attuned to the forces of creative love, dynamic good and the spiritual element of faith."

4. Now concentrate and reflect in the mirrorscope of

your soul the cosmic quality of OMNIPOTENCE—all-powerful, all energy and strength which is stored in the Cosmic Soul.

Say these words over and over until you feel this cosmic force of omnipotence charging every cell of your brain, body and soul with its cosmic totality of light, life and power.

"I concentrate my psychic powers now on the dynamic life currents which flow throughout the cosmos. I ask for life, energy, health, vibrant youth. This cosmic power now flows through my body and soul in a tidal wave of life-giving energy. Every cell of my brain and body is now bathed in the life-giving, healing, youthful, radioactive substance of universal power and omnipotence. I now grow strong, healthy and vital. My soul reflects the life force that will keep my mind and body functioning for a hundred years or more."

5. Now let the mirrorscope of your soul *reflect* the cosmic totality of power contained in the word OMNI-PRESENCE. Repeat these words until you feel charged with the dynamic cosmic life presence which stirs your every cell.

"I now partake of the cosmic quality of omnipresence, and reflect in the mirrorscope of my soul the quality of cosmic oneness with the life intelligence which stems from the soul of the universe and invests with life and power and intelligence every cell in the universal body. My consciousness now reflects the omnipresence of Cosmic Mind, giving me the power to be all-powerful, all pervading, all-knowing. I project my soul to any part of creation I choose. I explore time and space and know the secrets of the ages. I now concentrate my psychic power on receiving the cosmic vibrations that will cause me to receive psychic guidance from the higher forces ruling the universe. I release my soul from the confines of matter while I sleep and project my intelligence astrally to invisible realms where I may preview past historical events, consort with great souls from the past, and explore the mystic lands and hidden secrets of the ancient past. All life is now known to me through the omnipresence of Cosmic Mind."

6. Now attune your psychic nerve centers to the fol-

lowing thoughts and suggestions. As you hold these vibrant thought forms in the mirrorscope of your soul, they will be reflected in the soul of the cosmos, bringing you the benefits implied in the words used. Just as a still lake reflects the blue skies and white clouds, so too the mirrorscope of your soul will accurately reflect the dynamic and creative forces contained in these soul patterns of thought.

a) *Intelligence.* "I am now attuned to Cosmic Intelligence which guides me through my own soul pulsations."

b) *Health.* "My mind and body reflect the patterns of cosmic energy and dynamic power which give me life, health and vitality for every purpose in life. I channelize the healing power of the cosmic spirit which is ageless and timeless."

c) *Success.* "I now reflect in the mirrorscope of my soul the cosmic quality of success which is emblazoned in every cell and atom of the soul of the universe. I am successful in everything I undertake."

d) *Riches and abundance.* "I now hold in consciousness the psychic image of riches and abundance. I draw from the cosmic storehouse of universal riches the money, the goods, the abundance I need to fulfill my destiny perfectly. I possess riches of mind and spirit as well as material treasures. I attract to myself that which is opulent and abundant in every department of my life."

e) *Happiness.* "I now reflect in my higher psychic centers the universal overtone of joy and happiness. I am in tune with the universal rhythm of vibrant joy which cascades to earth in sun and rain, which causes the earth to come to life with shimmering, radiant beauty every springtime. This cosmic and universal rhythm from the soul of the universe also reflects in my life in perfect happiness, peace of mind and soul tranquility."

7. As you sit in the silence, focusing the light and intelligence of the Cosmic Soul in the mirrorscope of your soul, rise in consciousness to the fourth-dimensional realm of spirit. You do this by elevating your consciousness above the limited, physical and material third-dimensional sphere of life. When you elevate your true psychic consciousness into its proper cosmic realm of spiritual vision, you can truly claim the gift of seership and know secrets

of the past, present and future. The dimension of time, as we know it on earth, seems to disappear and we ascend to the spiritual mountain top where we have unlimited vision beyond the horizons of this earth.

Ascension is always symbolical of rising in consciousness to a more perfect, unlimited state of consciousness. When we ascend in an airplane to thirty thousand feet, we obtain a new perspective of the earth; all physical and material obstructions tend to fade away; mountains become flattened out, horizons come into view which we could not possibly see when on earth.

Your soul's ascension into the unlimited stratosphere of pure spirit frees you from the gravitational force of ordinary consciousness, and your soul rises on wings of inspiration into the lofty realm of cosmic illumination and psychic guidance.

Only when you rise above the gross third-dimensional sphere of animalism and materialism, into the lofty stratosphere of pure Cosmic Intelligence, which exists in the realm of the absolute, can your soul-mirror accurately reflect the pure, crystal-clear intelligence of the Cosmic Mind, which gives you psychic and intuitive guidance. Then you may know the hidden secrets of the universe and you may utilize the cosmic creative process to invent, compose, create and discover new forms of beauty, new products, and new combinations of elements to help elevate mankind to the realm of true cosmic greatness.

Summary of Chapter 8

1. The Cosmic Intelligence of the universe which contains all secrets of the past, present and future. How man may tap this intelligence through the mirrorscope of his soul.
2. Scientific proof that man has a soul and that he possesses psychic guidance through this soul power.
3. How to link your soul to the golden cosmic chain of universal soul radiation for greater power.
4. How Jesus used this Cosmic Soul power to per-

from his miracles of healing and psychic regeneration.

5. The six spiritual keys that help unlock the
mystical power within the soul of the universe
and cause it to reflect on the mirrorscope of your
soul.

6. How to attune your soul to the universal soul
power that can accurately guide you through
your psychic senses.

7. The regime for focusing your psychic powers
through the mirrorscope of your soul.

8. How to use psychic escalation of dynamic spiritual energy for performing miracles.

9. How to become omniscient, all-knowing, all-
wise, through the reflection of Cosmic Intelligence.

10. How you can use the powerful force of psychic
omnipotence, which will give you strength and
energy for health and bodily vigor.

11. How to use the cosmic totality of power through
psychic omnipresence, and charge your brain
and body with the cosmic life presence.

12. The dynamic and creative cosmic forces which
you can reflect in the mirrorscope of your soul
to bring you amazing benefits and unlock psychic
centers of your brain.

13. How to elevate your soul to the fourth-dimensional realm of spirit, where you can contact
the Cosmic Intelligence which gives you true
seership and the ability to know all secrets of the
past, present and future.

chapter 9

How to Use Psychic Somnambulism for Your Astral Projection

You can enter a state of psychic somnambulism where you can project your astral self to distant places and times.

You can know the secrets of ancients who lived in India, China, and Tibet centuries ago, by projecting your soul when you sleep, into the astral dimensions of time and space.

Psychic somnambulism will show you how to go into a sleeping state where you are conscious of exteriorizing your soul and exploring the realms of the invisible.

HOW YOU CAN RECEIVE THOUGHT FORMS FROM THE COSMOS

You can also use psychic somnambulism for astral reception of the thought forms, ideas and actual images that are in the Cosmic Memory bank of the universe. These may be from the minds of those living on the earth, or from the thought forms of the astral images of those who have been dead for years. Their thought forms still live and may often clothe themselves in the etheric doubles of their bodies, giving you the impression that you are in actual communication with the disembodied entities from other planes of consciousness.

The deathless, divine part of man is his immortal soul. In this lifetime it is clothed in a physical body, but the Cosmic Intelligence which makes man a thinking, breathing, loving, worshipping human being, is not contained in that fleshy prison. It is in his soul that man truly possesses the cosmic image of a vast intelligence which does not die when the body does, but exists in another dimension of time and space, as a conscious, intelligent entity, which has the ability to manifest itself as an etheric double to those who are still on earth when they are in the state known as psychic somnambulism in astral projection.

There are literally hundreds of authenticated cases of astral projection, where people have seen etheric doubles of those who once lived, or were still living, and talked with them, received guidance, warnings and other information, just as if the person were still alive and on the earth plane.

Very often, mothers, who are psychically attuned by an emotional and spiritual umbilical cord to their children, have these astral projections or psychic visions at the exact moment their children are threatened with danger.

AN ASTRAL PROJECTION FROM A SOLDIER IN VIETNAM

An instance of this type of astral projection was brought to my mind during the Vietnam war. A woman who had studied in my classes and knew a great deal about psychic phenomena, reported this case to me after it had happened. She dreamed she was in a place where there were vivid flashes of fire and loud sounds of artillery explosions. She saw men lying on all sides wounded and dying. As she walked through this scene of carnage she suddenly saw her son, lying on his back, his face covered with blood. She began to weep uncontrollably as she bent over him to comfort him. Her son opened his eyes and said, "Don't cry mom, I'll be all right."

She awakened, still weeping hysterically and sobbed, "Something has happened to Jimmy. I had a dream that he was wounded seriously." Her husband consoled her, telling her it was only a dream, and he noted the time, which they both later recalled. This woman did not go back to sleep that night.

A few days later she received a message from the war department telling her that her son had been seriously injured in an artillery barrage and was in a hospital. Later, when she checked with her son by letter to learn the details of his injury, he wrote her that his last conscious remembrance was of his mother and he had seen her face and told her that he would be all right. The time that he had been injured corresponded to the exact time of her psychic and astral dream!

YOUR SOUL CAN TAKE ASTRAL FLIGHTS WHILE YOU SLEEP

The soul of man is like an electro-magnetic force, which is able to pass through walls of steel and concrete. Just as mind is not imprisoned by the physical structure known as a brain, so too the soul is not held a prisoner by the physical body. It is a non-material force which has intelligence and obeys the laws of the fourth-dimensional world rather than those of the third dimension.

Your soul is capable of taking astral flights when you sleep; or of being projected in a state of psychic somnambulism, while you are awake, but in a trance-like state, where you are conscious of everything that happens to you in the astral flight.

You can have what you think are dreams, but which are actually astral projections to distant lands, even different ages and periods of history, where you talk to people who have been dead for centuries, where you receive information, guidance, and have intelligent conversations which you can later recall when you come out of your somnambulistic state.

MAN'S SOUL A PART OF THE COSMIC SOUL OF UNIVERSE

Man's soul is a part of the vast Cosmic Soul of the universe and possesses within its own structure, immortality—it will exist again in another dimension of time and space. It is the mystical, evanescent, etheric double which has unlimited powers of perception and knowledge, which man may tap when he enters that state of psychic somnambulism where his conscious mind is seemingly asleep, but his etheric double is always awake, always free of the body and always in a state of sensitive receptivity to the higher impulses that come from the Cosmic Soul of the universe. It is in this etheric medium of Cosmic Intelligence that man's soul may project itself to distant times and places, or into the dimension of the future, to know what is going to happen, and how to avert disaster, accidents and tragedies.

HOW A MAN'S LIFE WAS SAVED BY ASTRAL VISION

A man who had been in the U. S. Navy for a period of nearly four years, had to make a decision as to whether he should ship over for another four years or leave the navy.

This man was a radio operator on the battleship *Arizona,* and his sleeping quarters were directly over the powder magazine of the ship. One night he had an astral projection experience wherein a shell hit the powder magazine, killing practically the entire crew.

This dream troubled this man so much that when his time came to ship over, he decided to leave the navy. This was late in the summer of 1940. On December 7, 1941, a bomb from a Japanese plane attacking Pearl Harbor, fell into the smokestack of the *Arizona* exploding the stored ammunition aboard the ship. Nearly everyone was instantly killed!

This was an instance of astral projection of this man's soul into the future dimension of time and space, and it undoubtedly saved his life.

ASTRAL PROJECTION CAN BE TO THE PAST OR THE FUTURE

Astral projection can be in any dimension of time and space; past, present or future. As Einstein's theory of relativity proves, there is no time in cosmic spaces. *Time is man's invention.* The stream of consciousness, which is eternity, has inscribed upon its mystic scroll all past, present and future events. We can, in astral flight, go backwards in time, into any age or historical period, and know everything that has occurred in the past. Or we can project our souls forward, in the dimension known as the future, and be aware of events which will occur.

HOW A WOMAN TOOK ASTRAL FLIGHT TO ITALY

A woman I know had a strange astral dream one night in which she saw herself in Italy, being conducted to many places of interest. She recalled vividly an ancient castle, standing upon a promontory, looking out to sea. Although she had never been there before, this dream was so vivid that she wrote it down when she awakened. A year later she found herself actually visiting in Italy, and as a tourist guide was about to round a certain corner, the woman said, "There's a magnificent castle standing on a promontory looking out to sea around that corner." The guide smiled and said, "You must have been here before."

As they turned the corner there stood the ancient castle, exactly the way she had previewed it in her astral flight a year before!

THE TIME BARRIER DOES NOT EXIST IN THE UNIVERSE

We can see then, that the time barrier does not actually exist in the universe. We set these arbitrary limits with our own human consciousness as a frame of reference for the daily events of our lives. We are prone to break time up into three segments; past, present and future, but as far as the astral and psychic forces are concerned, time is nonexistent and is created only in man's consciousness. The psychic and astral experiences, whether they are projections from the past, or clairvoyant visions of the future, completely banish the time barrier. These psychic and astral experiences are able to hurdle the time barrier and project us backwards or forwards in time-consciousness.

HOW A DOCTOR AVERTED TRAGEDY THROUGH ASTRAL VISION

An instance of where astral vision occurred while a doctor was riding in his car, is proof that we need not be in a trance-like state to receive psychic or astral projections of future events.

This well-known doctor was driving behind a car in which there were four occupants. He had many opportunities to pass this car, but he didn't. He remained behind them, with a deep psychic conviction that the car would be involved in an accident. After a few miles, in which he continued to remain behind this car, it came to a crossroads, where a huge truck smashed into it, seriously injuring all four occupants. The doctor got out of his car and gave first aid to the injured, undoubtedly saving all of them from death.

SCIENTISTS PROVE THE EXISTENCE OF MAN'S SOUL

Dr. Rhine speaks of the psychological soul and believes that the mind is a separate and independent factor of what man calls the stream of consciousness.

Many famous men, including scientists, have done psychic research and have proved to their satisfaction that man possesses a soul. There exists within the human consciousness a non-material element that seems to be independent of the brain cells and man's nervous system and body chemistry. This spiritual entity, which we call the soul, is able to operate independently of matter and can exert spiritual energy against physical objects in a process known as psychokinesis.

A French scientist weighed a human being at the moment he died and found that he weighed a few ounces less at the moment of death, seeming to prove that some vital essence, such as the soul, left the body at the moment of death.

ASTRAL PROJECTION THROUGH A DREAM PROVED ACCURATE

Bill N. had an astral projection in which he accurately saw a future event in what seemed to be a vivid dream. He was an aviation student in life, and took two lessons a week at a nearby airfield. In his astral projection he was at the airfield about to get into his single engine plane when he saw a red plane flying against a vivid blue sky. Just as he was about to get into the cockpit of his plane with his instructor, the red plane crashed to the ground and burst into flames.

Bill N. was so shocked at this astral dream that he immediately awakened. He had never had any psychic experiences before and thought this was only a dream. He noted the time, and it was exactly fifteen minutes past three in the morning. He went back to sleep and the next day forgot his dream.

He arrived at the airport at noon. After a two hour lesson he came down safely, went into the small restaurant and had his lunch. Then he smoked a cigarette and finally went out onto the airfield again, preparing to go home. He looked up and saw a single engined red plane flying against a vivid blue sky; it was in that moment that his astral dream came back to him forcibly. Suddenly he heard the motor sputtering; the plane seemed to be in trouble and was heading for the airport. It crashed before his eyes and burst into flames! Bill looked up at the clock and it was exactly fifteen minutes past three.

A word of warning about inducing psychic somnambulism; you may feel strange sensations when you first begin this process of deliberately commanding your soul to leave your body while you are asleep. This may be a feeling of lightness or dizziness in your head, the body may suddenly feel light, and finally, in the last stages before you enter the somnambulistic stage, you may feel that you have *no body at all, only mind or spirit seems to exist.* It is in this last stage, as you seem about to lose consciousness that you will feel the *soul tugging,* like a kite on a string, as you finish the last stages of exteriorization—leaving the body you may then feel that you are soaring, like in an airplane, and you will struggle to hold onto consciousness, but it is better to let go completely, for your higher mind will retain parts of the experiences you have while your soul roams and explores out in the astral.

SOUL'S REMEMBRANCES OFTEN COME MASKED AS DREAMS

These soul's remembrances will be like vivid dreams, in which you will roam back and forth in foreign countries, and in past ages. When you wish to interiorize, or return to the body, your higher mind will cause you to go into a natural state of sleep and you will awaken at your usual time with only vivid recollections of fantastic dreams and unbelievable experiences while you were in the psychic somnambulistic state in the astral plane.

A PROGRAM FOR USING PSYCHIC SOMNAMBULISM TO INDUCE ASTRAL PROJECTION

1. When you are ready to go into the somnambulistic stage for astral projection, sit or lie down in a comfortable position. This can be in daylight or at night. If it is daylight the curtains should be drawn and the room darkened as if going to sleep. It is best to lock your door so you will not be disturbed while you are in your astral flight.

2. To put yourself into a half-sleeping, somnambulistic state, concentrate for a few moments on some bright object, like a crystal ball, or a watch that is a little above the line of vision suspended higher than your eyes.

3. Look at that object and keep saying to yourself over and over: "I am now going to enter a state of psychic

sleep, where I shall be aware of everything going on. I now still my conscious mind, so that no thoughts shall disturb it. I feel my eyes getting heavier and heavier; my conscious mind will be in a state of somnambulism, where I shall be asleep but my soul shall remember everything that I experience in astral flight. I now sleep—sleep—sleep—sleep."

4. You are now ready to go into the actual state of exteriorization, in which you will project your soul from your body. You will breathe deeply ten or fifteen times. Try to slow down the breathing process so that it is rhythmic and about half as fast as you would normally breathe in the waking state.

5. With your eyes closed and your mind now in a dreamy state, as it is between sleeping and waking, you will say to yourself over and over, "I now command my soul to project from my body out into time and space on an astral journey which shall take me into the past or into the future. I wish to recollect all experiences that my soul has while in this astral flight."

6. Now continue breathing deeply, and soon you will feel a sense of lightness come over your mind and body, as if you are drifting in space and about to lose consciousness. At this stage you might become frightened, for your heart will be beating in a loud and rather rapid rhythmic pattern, and you will be aware of sensations that you never felt before as the higher psychic centers of your brain open and are stimulated by the intense concentration and the flood of oxygen that hits your bloodstream. But do not become alarmed at this stage of psychic somnambulism; you are still in control of all your faculties and if you should become uncomfortable or fearful, you can immediately awaken from the slight stage of somnambulism you are experiencing.

If you wish to continue at this stage, you must now concentrate on your solar plexus, that region just below your lungs and above your stomach. You will feel that your soul is tied to that region by an invisible umbilical cord, as a child is tied to its mother when it is born. You will project up and outward from the solar plexus, visualizing your astral body, rising up—up—up, in a horizontal position,

118

just as if you were experiencing levitation above the earth. The sensation at this time may be that you are floating in space, weightless and without direction. You continue projecting this astral or etheric body up and out, and see it leaving your physical body. At this stage many people report that they seem to be suspended above their physical bodies and can actually see the room in which it lies, and the body lying on the bed or sitting in the chair. Then you make a move with your consciousness to pull the etheric body up, out of its horizontal position, into an upright position, and with one final thrust of your consciousness, you project the soul up and outward, all the time concentrating to achieve a total projection of the etheric body from the physical self.

7. When this final separation of the etheric double from the physical body comes, you may no longer be aware of any physical effort. You may suddenly enter the second stage of astral projection; that of seeming to lose consciousness in a deep, trance-like sleep. From this point on, you may have experiences which appear to your consciousness as vivid dreams. You may wander into the dimension of the past. Different periods of history, in which you may become another person, will be visited. Possibly you will even have a review of some former incarnation which your soul remembers and registers. There may be a pageant of faces upon the screen of your consciousness, a kaleidoscope of dramatic experiences, conversations and encounters with others, that will overpower your senses at this point.

8. When your etheric double has had enough of this astral wandering in time and space, in another dimension, it will know when to return to your body, which lies in a trance-like state in your bed. Sometimes you will retain a thread of consciousness which will cause you to feel you are having a vivid dream, and when you wish the etheric double to return to your physical body, give it a sharp command: "Return to my physical body immediately and retain a vision of all I have seen." This process is known as *interiorization*, where the etheric double—the soul—has returned to the sleeping body and awakened it in the pro-

119

cess of transition from the astral to the physical matter of the body.

9. The next session in which you practice astral projection use the same method for going into the somnambulistic stage, but give your etheric double specific directions as to what it shall do. You can consciously select a place or period in history which you wish to project to in your astral flight. It can be any given time, for remember, in the fourth-dimensional world all events are still registered in the realm of vibration. For example, you may choose ancient Greece, during the time of the building of the Parthenon; or you may send your astral double to Egypt when the great Pyramid of Ghiza was being built. You can send your astral double to ancient India or Tibet, and explore the mystic secrets of self-fulfillment; how you can be more creative in original projects; confer with geniuses of finance, or whatever else you may desire.

Astral flight to the Bahamas made this woman rich!

One member of our lecture group had an astral flight in which she saw herself living in a place, which seemed like an island, surrounded with water, and the shores lined with palm trees. She saw glistening white sand stretching away in the distance and few buildings or people. A year later she found herself going on vacation to the Grand Bahamas, and there were the palm-fringed shores of her astral dream! Some psychic urge made her buy undeveloped land near the ocean. She came back from her vacation, and kept up her small monthly payments on the land she had purchased. Now, several years later, the Grand Bahamas have had an astounding tourist growth and are rapidly becoming the Monte Carlo of the western hemisphere. The land this lady bought from a psychic prompting is now worth thousands of dollars and she can soon retire on the money she will get from its sale.

10. In some of your astral projections you can deliberately choose to visit certain periods of history and consort with famous historical personages. You might choose Queen Elizabeth the First, Shakespeare, Socrates, Rem-

brandt, Richelieu, Disraeli, Michelangelo, Columbus or Leonardo da Vinci. You can hold conversations with these illustrious souls, for their thoughts and inspirations are still existent in the dimension of time and space we know as the past. No vibration ever dies, and you may pick up the thought waves of these historical characters as if they were still alive and in the flesh. You may gain valuable information in this way that can help you in your present life.

11. You can receive astral thought forms in psychic somnambulism about some specific incident that you wish information about. In the Cosmic Memory vault there is a duplicate of all etheric images that have occurred since time began. The event you wish to experience or the information you desire, is locked up in that Cosmic Memory bank, and can be released to you while in a state of astral projection.

It may be some invention that you wish information about. You would go into your state of psychic somnambulism, and call upon the astral image of some inventor like Edison, Whitney, McCormick or Alexander Bell.

It may be a great story or theatrical drama you wish to write. You can call upon the astral projection of the minds of Balzac, Shakespeare, Dickens, Hawthorne, or O'Neill.

It may be some revelation in philosophy, and you can call upon the astral thought forms of a Socrates, Aristotle, Hume or Kant.

It may be an astral projection of a great art masterpiece or sculpture that you desire, and you can call upon the astral thought forms of a Michelangelo, Rodin, Gainsborough, Rembrandt, Leonardo da Vinci or Matisse. The original astral thought forms of these great artists still exist in the Cosmic and Astral Memory bank of the universe, and your soul can become the amplifier and projector which accurately images their inspired thoughts for your own creative efforts.

You may desire the astral projections of a great composer or inspired musician, and you can call upon the astral thought forms of a Beethoven, Chopin, Mozart, Bach or Puccini. If you wish to become a great singer, you can

121

choose the thought forms of Caruso, Mary Garden or Ezio Pinza.

12. Make it a point to study the lives of those souls you wish to contact in your astral projections; know their habits, their thoughts, their attitudes perfectly, so your ethereal double will more readily be magnetized by their vibrations. Then when astral thought forms come through to you from that person, you will be attuned to his astral wavelengths and attract him and his creative ideas into the orbit of your astral experiences.

13. You can receive automatic writing, painting, or other creative gifts through astral projection also. This form of astral telegraphy can occur while you are in a waking state, but one of psychic reverie, in which you call upon the thought forces of those you wish to contact for help in your own creative work.

This system of astral telegraphy works much as does the automatic writing done on a western union telegraph machine. The message is instantly transmitted by electrical impulses to another typewriter, even in a distant city, where the machine duplicates the message being written, just as if ghost fingers were doing the typing. Thousands of machines can be made to work instantly in different parts of the country through this transmission.

The stock market ticker tape works on this same principle, and appears simultaneously in offices throughout the country, where machines pick up the electrical impulses and translate them into written words and symbols.

AUTOMATIC WRITING OR PAINTING THROUGH THE ASTRAL FORCES

When you sit in the silence asking for automatic writing or painting, hold the idea in your mind which you wish information about, and be in a position where you can register the impulses that come through. To start with automatic writing, it might be best to use a pencil and paper, where you will not be involved with the mechanics of a typewriter—although later, you can transfer your activities to a typewriter with ease. Ask for definite information about some specific subject; or ask for the idea for a story or novel or scenario for television or movies. Then begin the process of writing by jotting down the letters of the alphabet to get the process started; when you feel the urge to write, begin to write no matter what comes through; jot it down, and let it continue as long as it wishes to. You might get a poem or a story, or merely some message that has no particular meaning, but in these first practice sessions the important thing is to keep on being a channel until you are able to control the process and receive messages that are significant and worthwhile.

You can ask specific questions about personal problems such as:

Should I move?
Where can I get the money I need to pay my bills?
Should I take this new job or stay where I am?
Can I trust the man who wants to go into business with me?
What can I do to improve my personality?
How can I make more sales of my product?

You can write down the subject or subjects that you wish information about at the top of your sheet of paper; then sit in a state of psychic reverie, holding your mind still, and let come through what will. You may be amazed at the information you receive.

HOW A BUSINESS CONTACT CAME THROUGH ASTRAL PROJECTION

One man who had this type of astral automatic writing, asked how he could improve his business and make more money. He sat in silence with a sheet of paper and a pencil in his hands, waiting for astral projections from some higher mind. The pencil wrote: "On the bus—on the bus —4 P.M." The message did not seem to make sense. However, he made a point of being on a bus at about 4 P.M. and he met a man who had been looking for him with a

123

business proposition that he wanted to make! The man who had received the astral projection through automatic writing looked at his watch and it was exactly 4 P.M.

Summary of Chapter 9

1. Psychic somnambulism used to project the soul to distant places and to receive thought forms, ideas and images from the Cosmic Memory bank of the universe.

2. Man's soul psychically attuned to other souls in the universe and receiving astral communications.

3. A mother who received astral projection from wounded son in Vietnam through psychic somnambulism.

4. Psychic and astral foreshadowing of future events which can be projected by the soul during astral flight.

5. Man's soul, a part of the cosmic soul of the universe and may be projected into time and space in astral flights.

6. An astral vision of the destruction of the battleship *Arizona* at Pearl Harbor.

7. The soul knowledge of the pattern of destiny and accurate prediction of it in psychic somnambulism.

8. How a doctor averted tragedy through using astral vision while he was wide awake.

9. The regime for using psychic somnambulism to induce astral projection for the soul's remembrances.

10. How to receive valuable information through automatic writing for soul and astral telegraphy while awake and conscious.

11. How to solve problems through automatic writing.

chapter 10

How to Release Psychic Energy for Power, Fame, Health and Security

Psychic energy flows through your brain and body and may be tapped for greater power to motivate every department of your life.

You can tap this higher psychic power for better health and youthful vitality.

You can release psychic energy to bring you fame and fortune and achieve security for your future life.

You will be able to tap this storehouse of psychic energy and receive divine intuition that will guide you in every move of your future life.

THE TREMENDOUS RESERVES OF PSYCHIC ENERGY WITHIN YOU

There are tremendous reserves of psychic energy which are stored in the brain and body cells and which you may tap to bring you into psychic attunement with the cosmic storehouse of dynamic power.

Just as we are able to store wheat and corn or freeze meat, vegetables and other foods for future use, so too the Cosmic Intelligence has a way of storing excess psychic energy which we may use for periods of emergency or when we wish to do something that is highly creative and productive.

You can channelize this vast storehouse of psychic energy when you desire mental, physical or spiritual power for any purpose in your life. You can build a great career and achieve fame and fortune by channelizing this tremendous reserve of psychic energy. You can build the vibrant, glowing, healthy energy in your body cells which will make you young and cause you to live a full, useful life to an advanced age, with all your faculties intact. You can achieve maximum security in this age of instability and fear, by tapping this higher psychic energy and it will surround you with a spiritual protective wall of vibrant and dynamic psychic force that can deflect danger, and protect you from all negative elements in your future.

MOST GENIUSES POSSESSED
THIS TYPE OF PSYCHIC ENERGY

Throughout history we find that most geniuses possessed this type of psychic energy.

There are five elements they all possessed which showed they all had a high degree of this psychic energy:

1. They all had a superabundance of vitality and energy and were able to do more creative work than three or four people.

2. They seemed to require less sleep than ordinary mortals, drawing upon some hidden inner spring of psychic energy that gave them power, diminished fatigue and caused them to recover quickly when tired or sick.

3. They had restless, searching minds which kept them on a perpetual quest for truth, beauty and inspiration which they could communicate to others through their great creative gifts.

4. They possessed a form of prophetic and psychic vision which gave them a perspective of eternity, not of a limited lifetime; thus they were able to tap more psychic energy for their creative efforts.

5. They all had vast springboards of psychic will which allowed them to transcend the ordinary limitations of their age and helped them overcome obstacles and discouragements on their road to fame and fortune.

HOW YOU CAN RELEASE PSYCHIC RESERVES
OF ENERGY THROUGH POSITIVE COMMANDS

The hidden reserves of power in the psychic cosmos can be summoned to all creation through one's positive commands. The acorn lying in the soil does not give up and die, but *commands the psychic force within its body to attract to itself the elements which sustain its life.* It becomes a giant oak tree because the reserves of psychic energy are stored within itself and are released by this power of positive commands.

You can release the psychic reserves of energy that are stored within your brain and body cells through the positive commands of *psychic will,* and they shall unlock tremendous power for every purpose in your life.

THE SIX FORMS OF PSYCHIC WILL
YOU MAY UNLOCK

1. The psychic will to health and long life
2. The psychic will to happiness and peace of mind
3. The psychic will to riches and success
4. The psychic will to love fulfillment and marriage
5. The psychic will for creative gifts and talents
6. The psychic will to find security and permanency.

The higher psychic centers of your mind are conductors of life force and energy. You can summon to the forefront of consciousness tremendous power in any department of your life by using these higher psychic centers and stimulating them each day with positive commands.

We shall now learn how to unlock the reserves of psychic power in each of the six departments of life given above by invoking the psychic will that taps these reserves of hidden power and energy.

HOW TO INVOKE THE PSYCHIC WILL
TO LIVE AND BE HEALTHY

The psychic will to live is inherent in every living cell of the universe. You can command the higher mind within to release dynamic, creative energy for your bodily health and for the preservation of your life.

1. Go into the *psychic silence* to invoke the higher will

to live, by stilling your conscious mind and opening the psychic centers of your consciousness through concentrating on the *picture of a perfect, healthy body*. Affirm the psychic will by saying over and over such positive statements as:

I am life and energy.
I am youth and vitality.
I am healthy and strong.
The life force within my body cells now flows strongly and heals me of all negative disturbances.
I now invoke the psychic will to live and accomplish my life work, and fulfill my right destiny.

2. When you are in the psychic silence seeking guidance you can write down a list of questions you wish answers to, that can serve as guidelines to better health. Ask this higher mind such questions as:

a) How can I implement the will to live?

b) What steps can I take to have good health and maintain it?

c) What diet should I follow to keep my body healthy?

d) How can I avoid dangers and threats to my safety and security?

e) How can I release greater stores of psychic life force and cosmic energy in my mind and body to keep my energy high and my body young?

f) What steps can I take to cause my body's organs to function perfectly without drugs?

g) How can I restore the energy of my mind and body when fatigued, without endangering my health?

h) How can I increase my life span beyond the three score and ten and maintain usefulness and efficiency until a ripe old age?

When you have invoked the psychic will to live and be healthy in this psychic session, sit and wait for answers to your questions. They may come through at that time or later when you are busy thinking of other things. There are a variety of ways in which this higher psychic mind will send through instructions about the questions you have asked.

You may be guided to read some book on health and diet which will furnish you with the information you desire.

You may receive a psychic prompting to eat certain basic foods which your body requires to furnish you with the vitamins, minerals and elements you need.

You may be guided intuitively to go to a certain climate in Arizona, California or Florida, where your health will benefit.

One woman I know had severe bronchial trouble and nothing seemed to help her. She learned how to go into the psychic silence and get information about problems that troubled her. While she was in this psychic state of sensitivity, she distinctly heard a voice within telling her to go to Phoenix, Arizona where she would find a healing power in the climate. She induced her husband to move to Arizona and within three months her health was so improved that she knew she had been guided correctly.

HOW TO INVOKE THE PSYCHIC WILL TO HAPPINESS AND PEACE OF MIND

1. Stir the psychic centers of the higher mind which control the energy and drive for happiness and peace of mind, by giving yourself positive psychic commands.

Repeat these or others that you make up, several times in the morning when you arise and face your day's work, and as often during the day as you need them to meet negative challenges and keep you in a high state of psychic energy and power.

I look forward with joy and expectancy to my good for this important day. I see only that which is a reflection of happiness, peace and radiance.

I reflect the happiness that is in the cosmic realm of transcendental joy and beauty. All nature is in rhythm with this force of vibrant, radiant happiness.

I tap the unending stream of cosmic life and channelize it this day to meet my every need. I am joyous and in control of all my life forces.

I overcome impatience, temper and anger which vitiate psychic energy and I substitute in their place patience, calm and confidence to meet every challenge that may arise this day.

2. Write down on little cards, which you can carry in your purse or wallet and look at several times a day, psychic energy boosters which will instantly release the flow of dynamic energy from the storage batteries of your psychic centers: I AM HAPPY. I AM LOVE. I COUNT MY BLESSINGS AND GIVE THANKS FOR MY GOOD. I AM LIFE. I AM INTELLIGENCE. I ATTRACT FRIENDS AND GOOD. I LOVE EVERYONE AND THIS PSYCHIC LIFE FORCE SUSTAINS ME. You can make up suitable psychic energy boosters to fit your own personal needs.

3. Utilize the psychic *law of good* in your relationships with other people. You will find that an unselfish desire to share your happiness and good with others will make you happier than the selfish desire to take from others without giving anything in return. Be good and do good, and you will discover that a radiant stream of happiness will flow into your life from the higher psychic storehouse of universal riches and goodness.

HOW TO INVOKE THE PSYCHIC WILL TO RICHES AND SUCCESS

We have learned elsewhere in our psychic studies that true riches are compounded of many diverse elements. The method for invoking the psychic will to bring you riches and success on every plane of consciousness is based on cosmic laws which are as universal and definite as the laws of gravity and capillary attraction.

1. As you sit in the mystic silence and ask for guidance, invoke the psychic will to riches by giving commands to your higher brain centers such as the following:

I affirm the law of universal riches and abundance. There is no poverty in nature, only plenty and good.

I now stimulate my higher psychic centers with a desire for riches.

I desire money to be used for good and constructive purposes.

I desire a house, car, jewelry, stocks, lands, and other physical and material forms of riches to give me comfort, security and luxury.

Psychic energy will now stimulate my mind with ideas and methods for bringing riches into focus in my future and present life.

2. Invoke the psychic law of magnetism to attract into your orbit of experience the persons, situations and conditions that will make you rich and successful. The image of these things must first be focused on the screen of your higher mind. Then you must invoke the *laws of desire and faith* to help stimulate these higher psychic nerve centers of your brain. You will be guided to making the right contacts, the right investments, the right moves in business, and you will attract the right people who can help you achieve the success you desire.

3. Use the *law of psychic acceleration,* which is used in nature when the cosmic spirit wants to quicken the seed in the soil to cause it to grow and produce a harvest. If wheat or corn were denied sunshine and water, it would soon die. The same way with your higher psychic centers; they must be fed a constant stream of refreshing, inspiring suggestions in your daily life, or they cannot cause the mental seed you plant to produce a rich harvest of plenty and abundance.

I call this the law of psychic acceleration for when you use it correctly it accelerates the process of enrichment and brings about instantaneous demonstrations of your riches. Jesus used this law of psychic acceleration when he multiplied the loaves and fishes and fed the multitude.

4. Invoke the psychic *law of transmutation;* change your ideas into gold; turn your services and labor into money and products which will enrich the world. Convert psychic energy into creative patterns of music, art, literature, inventions—that will bless and enrich all mankind, and you will in turn become blessed and enriched.

A woman of fifty, whose husband had died, needed to make a steady income, as she had been left no money. She had never been trained for business. She went into the psychic silence and asked for guidance, using this psychic method; she got her answer a few days later when walking down a street in New York she saw a sign that said, stenotype operating school. Some inner impulse caused her to go up the stairs to the office. She enrolled in a course in stenotype operating. A few weeks later, she met a friend who told her that a judge she knew wanted to engage a new stenotype operator as the present one was leaving to be married. This woman applied and got the job, despite her age. Her needs were met because she invoked this law of psychic transmutation. She converted service into money.

HOW TO INVOKE THE PSYCHIC WILL TO LOVE FULFILLMENT AND MARRIAGE

Every person was created to know love and fulfillment in marriage, to have a family of his own, and to indulge the God-given function of reproducing his own kind. The psychic will to love fulfillment can be stimulated through the following daily regime:

1. Use the psychic law of love which God has placed in His universe for all human beings to enjoy. If you short-circuit the psychic centers of your higher mind with the opposite emotion of *hate,* you will be denied the rich blessings of this divine emotion.

2. Express love as a daily emotion; love of your family; love of your co-workers, love of your community, your friends, your country. The higher psychic centers are stimulated to creative love when we have a sincere desire to do something for other people.

A woman of my acquaintance was so sick that the doctors gave her up to die. No medicine helped her, no therapy of any kind. She came into our lecture work and told me in a private interview that she had been filled with bitterness and hatred ever since her husband had left her several years before for a younger, more attractive woman.

I told her how to use the law of forgiveness and love and release her husband and the other woman to their own fate. She began to bless everyone she met; she radiated a loving smile, and a tolerant attitude towards the entire world. Within two months' time every symptom disappeared and, most amazing of all, a large tumor, which had developed in her abdominal cavity, began to shrink until X-rays revealed it was only as big as one's fist, and showed promise of completely disappearing! Truly, the psychic will which releases a healing power when one is in love, can work miracles in every department of life.

3. Affirm the psychic will for love fulfillment and marriage daily in statements to the higher brain centers. This will help release the psychic guidance that you need to lead you to the fulfillment of love. Say these affirmations every day, particularly when you arise in the morning; they will act as stimulating forces to the higher psychic centers of your brain.

I live every moment in the awareness of love as a healing, radiant force.

I release love to everyone I meet.

I remove the barriers of hate, jealousy, envy and resentment and fill my consciousness with the loving forces of sympathy, understanding, tolerance and forgiveness.

I strive today to be worthy of being loved.

I enthrone the cosmic image of universal love in my consciousness and strive to serve God and humanity with acts of love.

4. Choose the ideal qualities that you wish in your future mate and ask for psychic guidance to the person who best exemplifies those traits. This will set up a psychic attraction between you and the soul mate, which will cause your paths of destiny to finally cross.

HOW TO INVOKE THE PSYCHIC WILL FOR CREATIVE GIFTS AND TALENTS

There is a cosmic plan for every living person on the face of the earth. Indeed, this cosmic plan extends to all forms of cellular life, including animals, birds, insects and growing plants or trees.

By invoking the psychic will for bringing out your own creative gifts and talents your life can suddenly blossom with all kinds of wonderful expressions of talent. You can paint pictures, write stories or plays, compose songs, invent new forms of modern mechanical wonders and discover new scientific secrets, formulas and combinations of ideas for creating new products.

The great geniuses of history had multiple talents; Benjamin Franklin was not only a great orator, statesman and writer, but he was a skillful inventor as well, having discovered and invented the first bifocals.

Churchill was a statesman, author, painter, and orator, who could sway millions with his inspirational gifts.

Eisenhower was a great general, a famous president, a writer of note, as well as an artist of great talent.

Leonardo da Vinci not only painted and wrote, but also invented the world's first airplane.

These great geniuses all knew how to instinctively tap the power of the *psychic will* which guided them to the development of unusual skills and talents.

1. To invoke your own psychic will for creative gifts and talents, go into the creative silence for at least an hour a day and make out a questionnaire in which you ask your higher psychic centers:

a) How can I more readily release my own hidden potentials and develop my gifts and talents?

b) Where can I go to seek out sources of knowledge and specialized skills that will help me in my own career?

c) What cultural processes should I follow to refine my own personality and raise my own standards of conduct and creativity?

d) What creative channels should I seek out to express my own creative talents?

e) How can I meet important people who will help me achieve my cultural and creative goals in life?

f) What steps should I take to build up a strong, magnetic personality which will make me a leader among men?

g) How can I develop my intellect and become a truly superior creative being?

HOW THIS PSYCHIC POWER GIVES YOU THE ANSWERS

When you have finished your psychic concentration, you may go about your business and be confident that the psychic will must manifest for you the creative gifts that you desire. You will receive direct guidance or be led to a book, which will tell you a formula for developing the talent you wish, or you will meet some person who will make it possible for you to achieve creative fulfillment.

HOW PSYCHIC WILL CHANGED A WOMAN'S LIFE

A housewife in the Midwest once told me how she had used this type of psychic guidance to change her life from one of drabness and mediocrity to a glamorous, brilliant social life where she became one of the most sought after hostesses in Washington, D.C. She was married to an attorney and he was content to live an ordinary life, making an ordinary salary, in a small home on the outskirts of a small city. This woman began to use the psychic will intuitively, which caused her to enroll in a public speaking course; to study personality development, and other related subjects. She began to visualize herself being a hostess in Washington, D.C., but she saw no possible way for making the long, difficult jump from her life of obscurity to one of social prominence in the nation's capital. However, she kept up her cultural and artistic studies. She read every book she could find on politics and examined the lives of the great men and women who had achieved outstanding success in that field. She subscribed to national magazines which kept her abreast of the times and made her conversant with what was going on in the theater, the literary world, medicine, science, business and economics. She had a driving intuitive urge to perfect herself in manners, in entertaining at social functions, and being charming and attractive to people.

One day she read that a famous senator from her state would be paying a visit to their city to make an appearance at a college. She found out where he would be staying; her instinct made her write him, inviting him to dinner at her home. She was so fascinating as a hostess that this senator told her husband before the evening was over that he must run for political office, as the other senator from their state was retiring owing to age and illness, and he felt this man, with the charming social wife could easily win the office.

Within a matter of months the voters went to the polls to pick a new senator for their state. This man, whose wife had developed her psychic will for greater creative gifts, was elected. They moved to Washington, D.C. and this woman became one of the most popular hostesses in the Capitol! If this woman had not been aware of her higher psychic will it is doubtful if her husband would ever have been inspired to make the effort to win high public office.

Commence using the cosmic law of involution and evolution to help your higher psychic centers release creative power for your life. If you put into your consciousness knowledge, power, wisdom, cultural and artistic riches, you will be involving in your psychic mechanism the creative impulses which will be released in a floodtide of creative gifts and talents. Read good books, listen to classical music, as well as the modern sounds, which too often are not of high quality; look at magnificent art treasures in the public galleries; imprint upon your higher psychic centers

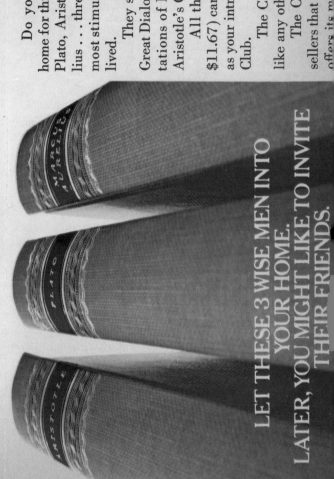

Do you have room in your home for three wise men? They are Plato, Aristotle, and Marcus Aurelius . . . three of the wisest, wittiest, most stimulating minds that ever-lived.

They still live . . . in the Five Great Dialogues of Plato, the Meditations of Marcus Aurelius, and Aristotle's On Man in the Universe.

All three books (regularly $11.67) can be yours for only $1.00 as your introduction to the Classics Club.

The Classics Club is quite un-like any other book club.

The Club does not offer best sellers that come and go. Instead, it offers its members a chance to stay

LET THESE 3 WISE MEN INTO YOUR HOME.
LATER, YOU MIGHT LIKE TO INVITE THEIR FRIENDS.

ENJOY THE COMPANY OF THREE OF THE WISEST MEN WHO EVER LIVED

(Continued from other side)

The selections themselves are remarkable values. They are carefully printed on expensive paper stock. They are hard-bound in matched sand-colored buckram, worked and stamped in crimson, black, and genuine gold. And through direct-to-the public distribution, we are able to offer our members these deluxe editions for only $3.89 each, plus shipping.

Interested? We will send you the first three selections, Plato, Aris-

the beauty in nature, and you will find that gradually these higher vibrations will become caught up in the warp and woof of your tapestry of dreams, giving you a perfect cosmic blueprint by which to build your life.

HOW TO INVOKE THE PSYCHIC WILL TO FIND SECURITY AND PERMANENCY

Everyone is searching for future security in a world that seems to be transient and impermanent. You cannot depend on the outer world of change and confusion for this form of security. We are now living in one of the most progressive ages in history, where man has conquered the earth and is now reaching out to conquer space. We have the greatest riches of any country in the world, and yet we have more insecurity, more mental breakdowns, more juvenile delinquency, crime, dope addiction and sickness than in any other period of history.

What is the reason for this astounding paradox?

It is because man has not found the true internal security which his soul seeks. Only when he turns to the higher psychic mind within and searches for guidance to the true values of life can he hope to overcome the problems of war, depression, poverty, and political strife. You can learn how to release this storehouse of psychic energy in your own life and set it in order, and gradually, like ripples on a stream, this psychic power will radiate into the lives of others, bringing them into a state of universal order, harmony and fulfillment.

1. Make it a point to withdraw from the physical and material universe for at least half an hour a day and go into the psychic silence, where you contemplate on the true power sustaining all life. Know that this is a spiritual power and that you can tap cosmic energy by keeping your mind and emotions intact, and not receive psychic shocks from the violence and chaos in the outer world. Learn to repeat this formula for handling all disturbing and disruptive forces that might cause you to be upset.

137

This too shall pass away.

Write these words down on a card which you keep in your purse or wallet and say them whenever you feel unhappy, insecure or excessively burdened by problems.

2. Affirm these powerful statements which express your psychic will to security and permanency. You can do this upon arising in the morning and as many times a day as you feel the need, using the ones that fit your own particular case.

I now ascend the spiritual mountain top where I am rising above the gravity pull of earth. My problems, fears and worries now fade away and I peer into the unlimited horizons of eternity, finding only peace, happiness and security.

I enter the inner realm of my cathedral of the soul, where I now restore my psychic energy at the divine altar of good, love, beauty and harmony. I am healed of all friction, discord and disunity in this peaceful realm of the spirit.

I now draw upon my higher psychic mind for my daily strength and power and am able to weather the storms of life. I am strong and vibrantly alive and able to dissolve all problems and anxieties in the golden light of truth and faith.

3. A very wonderful source of psychic and spiritual energy is the twenty-third Psalm. Repeat this whenever you feel a sense of fear, loss or insecurity. The ninety-first Psalm is another excellent one for this purpose.

4. Build your life on the permanent psychic and spiritual values which survive the crash of matter; empires and kings fade away, and the conqueror's sword turns to rust, but the inspired words of the poets, the magnificence of classical art and music, the great ideas in philosophy, the beauty and inspiration of good literature, the spiritual words of the prophets—these are the true sources of divine and cosmic inspiration, and they survive throughout eternity. They are the only true sources of sustaining power

and offer the only permanency in a world of flux and change.

Summary of Chapter 10

1. How to tap the vast reserves of psychic energy in the brain and body and use it for power, fame, health and security.
2. How geniuses throughout history used this psychic method to create their great works.
3. The power of positive commands to release this psychic reserve of energy for creative purposes.
4. How to use the six forms of psychic will to achieve your fulfillment of destiny.
5. The will to live, how it stimulates the life force.
6. The psychic will to happiness and peace of mind.
7. How you can invoke the psychic will to riches and all forms of success.
8. How one woman invoked this psychic will to create financial independence for herself after her husband had died.
9. How to invoke the psychic will to love fulfillment and marriage.
10. How to invoke the psychic will for creative gifts and talents and achieve creative expression.
11. How you can invoke the psychic will to find security and permanency in your life.

chapter 11

How You Can Solve
Your Daily Problems
Through Psychic Mediumship

You can become a channel through which Cosmic Mind manifests itself in every department of life.

A medium is one who is able to tap a higher form of psychic power which transcends his own conscious, volitional mind and uses that power for constructive good.

If you are beset with problems that you cannot solve with your conscious mind, you can learn how to turn to this form of psychic mediumship and use it every day to solve problems, to guide and direct you into channels of constructive good.

A tree does not have to ask help from human beings for drawing nourishment from the soil and creating branches, bark, leaves, flowers and fruit. It uses a form a psychic mediumship to contact the Cosmic Mind of the universe which knows all secrets and can show creation how to achieve fulfillment.

MANY PERSONS USE PSYCHIC MEDIUMSHIP
TO SOLVE PROBLEMS

Psychic mediumship is used by thousands of people to solve their daily problems and overcome obstacles that stand in the way of destiny fulfillment. Many times people do not know they are tapping a stratum of higher psychic power and receiving thoughts and inspiration from some higher source. This psychic help may come from the minds of other people or it can come through their own higher psychic centers.

You can harness the powers of psychic mediumship to

help yourself overcome problems in your personal life, or to assist friends and relatives in their lives.

HOW TO USE PSYCHIC STIMULATORS

When you have chosen the particular problem or problems which you wish Cosmic Mind to help you solve, you can use the following six psychic stimulators to aid you in the process of mediumship. You will ask your higher mind questions prefaced by one of the following six psychic stimulators.

1. Why?
2. How?
3. Where?
4. What?
5. When?
6. Who?

Now we are ready to take up the main problems that beset humanity. Find the particular problem that disturbs you and which you wish to solve through psychic mediumship. Then follow the procedure given under the classification for that particular problem, sitting in the silence and stimulating the psychic centers of your brain until you receive the information you want from the higher, Cosmic Mind of the universe.

Problem No. 1   Lack of Money,
Poverty and Related Problems

Go into psychic reverie through the method you have previously studied. Have with you a piece of paper on which you write down the main problems upon which you wish advice and guidance. In this instance you will probably write something like the following:

How can I solve my money problems? I need the sum of . . . . (Put down the amount you need for this particular time) and I would like to know how

141

I can make some more money to pay my bills and get out of debt. (Or you might say, to pay off the mortgage on my house, to clear my car, to buy furnishings, etc.)

Now go into a period of at least a half hour of psychic concentration on this particular problem. Use the six psychic stimulators to stir the higher psychic power within your own mind into dynamic action. Ask the Cosmic Mind to give you the answers to the following questions, prefacing them with one of the six psychic stimulators.

1. Where can I get the money I need?
2. How can I convert what I have into cash?
3. What talents do I have which I could develop for making extra money?
4. Who should I see to help me solve this problem?
5. Why am I having lack and limitation, and what can I do to be successful and rich?
6. When will I be able to solve this problem?

An insurance salesman's experience

An example of how psychic mediumship works to help you solve your problems is that of an insurance salesman who once came to my lectures in New York City. He lacked the ability to conclude a sale, and he could not make the money he needed to keep himself and his family. He learned of this method of psychic mediumship and he went into the silence, used the psychic stimulators, and the following information came through:

Enroll in an evening course in public speaking. Your personality lacks magnetism, confidence and poise. Be more dynamic, learn to smile; crack a joke. Don't talk about insurance but about the prospect's family, his work, his interests and hobbies. Sell insurance as an afterthought. Instead of pounding directly on the benefits to be gained, dwell on the security of his family, the education of his children,

142

and the bright future that beckons him and his loved ones.

Within three months' time this man's insurance sales jumped 25 percent. In a year's time he was selling more insurance than anyone else in his company and his progress continued, until he won advancement and higher pay, as well as bigger commissions from his sales.

If this man had tried desperately with his conscious mind to solve his problem, he would have become entangled with all kinds of arguments and subconscious obstacles. His higher psychic vision knew how to get directly to the point and advise him instantly what he should do to help him increase sales.

Problem No. 2   Relating to Illness
and Accident

There are times in every life when sickness and accident are apt to strike. No matter how psychically attuned we may be to this higher mind, we still live in world where there are sources of danger to life and limb, and where we may become sick from any one of a hundred causes.

You can tap this higher psychic mind to keep you well in most instances, but if you should have accidental illness or misfortune, you can turn to this higher psychic force and ask for guidance.

Sit in the silence using the instructions given above, and write down on a piece of paper the questions you wish to ask the higher Mind, using the six forms of psychic stimulators given:

1. Why am I sick?
2. How can I overcome this illness?
3. Where should I go for help?
4. What causes my illness and what should I do to overcome this health problem?
5. When can I expect to be restored to normal health?
6. Who shall I see to achieve my healing?

Of course you may use any combination of questions, the above are merely given as a guide. When you have some specific form of ailment you can ask specific questions for direct action in your health problem.

For example, if you know you have headaches, or high blood pressure, or bronchial trouble, your questions might take on a different form:

What causes my headaches?
How can I overcome them?
Who should I see about getting rid of my headaches?
What diet should I follow?
Or, if you suffer from bronchial trouble you might ask:
Where should I live to overcome my bronchial trouble?
What diet is best for my condition?
Who can help me with this health problem?
What is causing this bronchial condition?

A healing of a mysterious allergy

A specific complaint which was asthmatic and bronchial in nature, afflicted a member of my New York lecture group. For years she had suffered from violent asthmatic attacks in which she could hardly get her breath. She went to many doctors and they told her she had an allergy. To find what the allergy was she took over one hundred different shots made up of dust, pollen, dog hairs, various types of food, and other substances they thought she was allergic to, but nothing seemed to work.

When she learned how to go into psychic reverie to help herself, she received a short and simple answer: she had been in love with another man when she married her husband, but the man made a very small salary and her husband could give her more security, so she married a meal ticket and let the only love she had ever known go out of her life. The psychic voice within told her to stop resenting her husband and thinking about her lost love. She was urged to begin to love and respect her husband and make him happy.

This woman faced the facts of her life and followed the advice given by her higher mind. Within two months time her asthmatic and bronchial condition completely disappeared and she was healed!

Problem No. 3   Relating to Business
Matters and Relationships

Under this classification you may list any and all problems that relate to your work, to failure, to friction in your business environment, problems of investment and other matters that relate to business, success, money and your future.

You might ask the following questions, using the six psychic stimulators:

Why am I not successful in my business activities?
What work am I best suited to doing?
Who will help me get into my right work?
How can I best use my hidden gifts and potentials?
Where can I go to be in my right environment?
When will my investments be better and how can I improve them?
What stocks should I invest in?
How can I find the capital to expand my business?

A healing of job unemployment

You can extend this list of psychic questioning to as many questions as you wish. Of course, after you have written down your questions you should wait and examine each question, to see if a psychic answer comes immediately. As a rule, I have found that the answer and guidance will often come through at another time.

One instance of this type that I know of, was a man who was a painter. He worked for a contractor in southern California, and when there was lots of work, he prospered. But when it was a lean season he was laid off, but still had

145

to support his wife and five children. It was during such a lean season that his psychic guidance come through in a vision. In a half-sleeping state he saw a small truck with his name written on the side, and the words, Painter and Decorator, No Job Too Big or Too Small. When he came out of his psychic reverie he took the last few hundred dollars he had, bought a second-hand panel truck, had it painted as he saw in his vision, and had cards printed giving his name and telephone number. In a short time job offers poured in, and soon he had to have four assistants to help him. In one year's time he became one of the best known painters and decorators in the valley, and had four trucks, and was on the way to buying a beautiful home with a swimming pool!

The higher psychic mind within knows even better than you do *your hidden potentials* and how to guide you to success and riches in your own field.

What if an answer comes through in psychic meditation or later, when you are given the answer to what you should do, and it is different from what you would normally expect? Should you follow psychic guidance blindly and depend on it, or let your own conscious preferences guide you? As a rule, your higher psychic mind will not guide you in a direction that is contrary to your own preferences and potentials. It knows what you are capable of doing, and you will seldom go wrong by following your psychic instructions.

Problem No. 4   The Overcoming
of Personality Disorders, Self-
Consciousness, Inferiority and
Inadequacy

Personality disorders may be of many different types; you must select your own particular problem and state it clearly by writing it down. You may want to become more dynamic, magnetic and forceful. You may want to become a good salesman, a leader of others, an executive.

Assuming you want to overcome the personality disorders listed under problem number four, you might write down these questions, using the six psychic motivators:

146

How can I overcome self-consciousness and inferiority?

What steps should I take to become dynamic and magnetic?

Who will help me achieve my goal of being a strong, dominant personality?

What books should I study to achieve personality integration?

Where can I go to learn better speech, diction and rhetoric?

When will I be ready to present my new personality to the world and achieve my destiny?

How can I become a better salesman?

Where can I go to meet important people who will help me achieve my goals in life?

You can have a sheet of paper before you as you go into psychic reverie and ask your questions, and then jot down any answers that might come through.

If no definite answers come in psychic reverie go about your business and you may later be guided to a book that will give you needed information, or you may meet a person who knows the answer and offers to help you; or your own psychic centers may be stimulated to do research and study that will give you the solution to your problem.

Problem No. 5   Overcoming
Negative Habits, Smoking,
Drinking, Procrastination,
Laziness, Gambling and Excessive
Spending

There are many other negative habits than those listed under this problem. You know your own habit patterns, and if they are harmful or negative, you can take steps to change them through psychic mediumship.

Put on your list, when you go into the psychic silence, the habit or habits which you wish guidance in overcoming, and then make out a list of questions to stimulate your higher psychic nerve centers, based on six psychic stimulators. The list might read as follows, choosing the habit of smoking.

What harmful effects, if any, can come to me through my smoking?
What steps can I take to stop smoking?
Where will I go to get help to overcome this habit?
How should I proceed to stop smoking?
When can I expect results?
Who can help me solve this problem of smoking?
What benefits can I expect in the future?

Each of the negative habits given above—smoking, drinking, procrastination, laziness, gambling and excessive spending—can be handled the same way through psychic mediumship. After all, habits that are negative and destructive are due to some negative condition within the human psyche. You cannot handle them through force; you need higher guidance to be able to achieve any kind of mental strength and emotional stability. The higher psychic mind, which knows what is good or bad for you, is equipped to handle these problems or any others you may have.

Problem No. 6   Friction and
Discord in the Home and Work

Sometimes friction will arise in your home or place of business and seemingly there is nothing you can do but bear it. Your higher psychic vision can be enlisted in such an instance and it will know many solutions to this trying problem.

Why should this problem exist in my life?
What can I do to overcome friction and discord in my marriage?
How can I get along better with people at my place of business?
What steps should I take to get along better with other people?
How can I change my personality to avoid being short-tempered, angry and resentful?
Who is to blame for these irritating situations?

Let thoughts bombard your mind without trying to control them, for your higher psychic centers may send through a solution in this manner.

Or you may select some conscious solution to your problem and hold it in your consciousness, asking for more information on the subject.

As you ask these or other questions about your problems, the psychic centers will become stimulated, giving you many forms of stimuli for carrying out constructive action.

How marital friction was solved

One woman I know who used this psychic method for overcoming friction and discord in her marriage, seemed to be in an unsolvable problem. She didn't know which way to turn. She had married a man who had a widowed mother with no home of her own. After the marriage this mother moved in with her son and daughter-in-law. She was foreign born and had her own ideas about how to run a home, and resented the fact that her son had married a girl not of his own national origin. All went well until after the first child was born, then the grandmother insisted on rearing the child as she would have in her own country. Everything she did went against the younger woman's grain, and soon she and her husband were quarreling constantly and her marriage seemed threatened. The mother wanted to bring the child up speaking her national language; the girl wanted her child to speak English, but the mother refused to speak English in the child's presence. Things went from bad to worse until this young woman sought out help at my lectures and learned how to solve problems through psychic guidance.

She went into psychic reverie and asked her higher mind questions pertaining to her problem, then went about her affairs, waiting for the solution.

One day she got her answer in a letter that came from her husband's brother, who lived in Chicago. He said he was marrying a girl of his own nationality and he wanted the mother to come to his wedding, if possible, and to make her home with them in the future. As this was a younger son, the woman was delighted at his coming marriage. She made the trip to Chicago, and began making preparations to live with the newly married couple wishing to help them rear their first-born according to her standards. The solution to this problem lay outside the province of the girl's own actions, but the higher psychic intelligence which guided her to do nothing but wait, was already at work with a solution that would be suitable to everyone.

Problem No. 7   Overcoming General
Unhappiness, Moodiness, Depression
and Anxiety States

Many times we are troubled in life with vague, general moodiness and depression, which leads to a state of chronic unhappiness. Nothing definite seems to be wrong, but we seem to suffer from general lassitude and lack of interest in anything in life. It is in such times that we seem to have no definite purpose in living, and our chronic moodiness and depression can affect everyone around us.

When you write out your list of questions, using the six psychic stimulators, your questions might be like this:

Why am I so moody and depressed?
How can I become happy and remain happy?
What am I doing that is wrong in my life?
Whom should I associate with to help me?
When can I get out of this depressing environment?
Where can I go to find the pattern of life I desire?
How can I find security in my life?
What causes my general lassitude?

As you dwell on each question, the answer may come in psychic reverie. You might get flashes of sudden information, which you should note when it comes through. You might get no definite answer in that session, but later, when you least expect it, some definite answer will come through. Many times you will be led to a book for the answer; or a friend may tell you something which starts you on a quest that brings about a solution of your problem.

Problem No. 8   Relating to Love
and Marriage Failure

There are many classifications to problems that relate
to love and marriage, and your higher psychic mind knows
how to solve all of them. When you try with your own
conscious mind to seek a solution to emotional problems
of this nature, you are too close to the problem to see it
objectively. You must turn with confidence to this higher
mind within and let it guide you if and when such troublesome problems arise in the romantic department of your
life.

Be sure, however, that you state your problem clearly
when you go into the silence to ask for guidance. To assist
you, here are some of the main problems relating to love
and marriage:

Not being able to win the beloved.
Not knowing for sure whether you have chosen the
right person in marriage.
Clashes in temperament between you and the loved
one.
Jealousy because of infidelity in the marriage state.
Problems relating to sexual incompatibility in mar-
riage.
In-law problems of various kinds.
Financial problems which threaten marriage security.
Parental objections to the marriage.
Racial, religious or educational differences that
threaten the romance or marriage.

HOW TO USE PSYCHIC STIMULATORS
TO HELP YOU

Put these questions into your psychic mind:
Why am I having these problems in my romance?
Who is at fault for my problems?
What can I do to change this distressing condition?
Who will be best for me in marriage?
Where can I go to find my true marriage partner?

What qualities should I seek in my future mate?
Where should I go to seek out fulfillment in love and marriage?
What steps can I take to make my marriage a success?
How can we solve this problem without resorting to divorce?

How a woman had psychic guidance in her marriage

A woman who had a very disturbing problem in her marriage, which concerned infidelity on the part of her husband, was so violently upset when she discovered this, that she was determined she would divorce her husband. She came to one of my lectures and later told me that her psychic answer came through while she sat there listening to me. One phrase I used triggered something in her higher psychic mind which gave her the solution. I was telling about life and how there are two sides to everything; light and dark; good and bad; love and hate; beauty and ugliness; riches and poverty, and how very often a situation presented the negative side of the coin, but all we had to do was reverse the coin and we would instantly see the positive side. She then had a psychic flash that the other side of the coin of love, which might have caused her husband to stray from the home in search of another romance, could have been her own indifference and neglect and selfishness.

With this beginning from her psychic flash, she returned home with a totally different viewpoint. She examined both aspects of marriage, and found that she had erred also in letting herself become slovenly around the house, in putting on unsightly weight, and in allowing the romantic spark to die. She began to change these conditions. Instead of getting a divorce, she followed through with a positive program of changing herself, improving her appearance, lighting the light of romance once again, and finally she completely won her husband back from the other woman and went on to a happy, beautiful relationship in her marriage.

Problem No. 9   Social Problems,
Lack of Popularity, Lack of Magnetism,
Loneliness and Other Related
Problems

Your particular social problem may be different from
those stated above. You might want to become socially
prominent, and feel that you are unable to achieve recognition because of lack of financial or educational background; or you may be in a situation where you have to
entertain people for business reasons, when you would
rather live a secluded life. No one is equipped to give you
advice on your particular problem but your higher psychic
centers. Write down the main problem that bothers you,
and then go into the psychic silence and let your mind
receive the answers to the following psychic stimulators
that you ask of this higher mind.

Why am I unpopular socially?
How can I become more magnetic and charming?
What can I do to make people like me?
What books should I study to become more magnetic?
Who can help me achieve popularity and social
graces?
How can I overcome loneliness?
Where can I go to safely meet the right kind of
friends?
What qualities should I develop to make me well
liked?
How can I overcome my feelings of being anti-social?

During your psychic meditation you may receive many
impulses of what you should do; how you can change
yourself for the better; whom to seek out for guidance or
help, and you can make your decision as to your course
of action for the future.

How a young lady came alive socially

I remember one young lady who came to me once for
personal counselling, who was rather mousey and drab in

appearance. She was young, about twenty-two, but romance did not seem to seek her out and she suffered from loneliness and unhappiness. I analyzed her and told her that she could be very striking in appearance if she would change the style of her hair and dress. I also told her she could enroll in a short course in modelling, to learn how to walk and stand, and wear her clothes. She had been driven to seeking out help by her desire for a better life, and she knew nothing about psychic guidance or metaphysics. I also told her that she could go into psychic reverie and let her higher mind guide her as to the steps she should take to completely remake her life. I gave her the full program as presented in this book.

She left and I heard no more about her, until one day weeks later, while walking on Fifth Avenue in New York, I saw a glamorous, platinum blonde, stylishly dressed, coming down the street, and every head was turning to see her. When she came closer to me, I still did not recognize her until she stopped and greeted me. It was the drab, mousey girl of the interview. She had changed so radically that I did not recognize her. She then told me that a whole new series of experiences had opened to her when she began to receive psychic guidance from her higher mind. "You started me on the road to personal awareness of my hidden potentials," she told me. "Then I realized that I had to do something about it. Now I have an opportunity to go to England as a representative of a cosmetic firm, and your advice changed my entire life."

Summary of Chapter 11

1. How the higher psychic mind can help overcome all personal problems.
2. The six psychic stimulators to help your mind stir up psychic energy for solving your problems.
3. How you can overcome problems relating to lack of money, poverty and limitation.
4. How an insurance salesman increased his sales 25 percent through this method.

5. Solving problems relating to sickness and accident through psychic mediumship.
6. A lady who suffered from bronchial conditions shown how to achieve a cure through psychic mediumship.
7. Business problems that are overcome through this method.
8. A contractor uses psychic mediumship to build a fortune.
9. Personality defects, bad habits such as smoking and gambling, and other negative forces overcome through psychic mediumship.
10. Psychic mediumship helps overcome unhappiness, moodiness, depression and psychic states of anxiety and worry.
11. Romantic and marital problems yield to this psychic force and are solved.
12. A woman wins back her husband's love through psychic guidance.
13. A girl's entire personality changed from plain and drab, to being magnetic and charming through this form of psychic guidance.

chapter 12

How to Increase Your Level of
Psychic Awareness for
Your Benefit

There is a magic genie within your mind which you can summon to carry out your every command.

You can release unlimited psychic power when you are aware of this slumbering, inner force that can change the world for you.

By increasing your level of psychic awareness you can cross over that mystical threshold between dreams and reality and summon up the power to achieve any type of success you can visualize.

You will no longer depend on your conscious mind and your five physical senses for achieving fulfillment.

How to make a psychic portfolio

Before you can increase your level of psychic awareness however, it is necessary that you create, what I term the *psychic portfolio* within your own consciousness, from which your higher mind can draw the images and thought forms of what you are trying to create in your own life.

Let us examine how this principle works in the cosmic realm, through what we call psychic awareness in nature.

A kernel of wheat does not seem to be very important for visibly it is only a tiny speck of matter. Yet, it possesses within its substance all the elements that can create illimitable crops of wheat to nourish humanity for generations to come. It might be said that this speck of wheat is nature's psychic portfolio, in which is stored the cosmic blueprint for all wheat that will ever be produced for all time.

In stock market speculation a broker often speaks of a

portfolio of stocks. This refers to a diversified group of valuable stocks which make up a person's total investments. It might consist of stocks in General Motors, Sinclair Oil, Dupont Chemicals, General Electric, Boeing Aircraft, Trans World Airlines and International Business Machines.

To increase your level of psychic awareness for all success, I would like you to think that there is a psychic portfolio also within your consciousness. In this inner, invisible realm are stored all secrets, all ideas, all valuable combinations and formulas, all knowledge and all power.

To draw upon this psychic portfolio you need merely predetermine what it is that you want in your life and then go into psychic reverie and concentrate on receiving the information you desire directly from this higher psychic mind within.

When you want to produce a crop of wheat, you must plant the seed first within the soil and then await its maturity for the crop you wish to harvest.

This law of psychic phenomena works in nature to produce the outward physical and material equivalents of all the things that are stored in the psychic portfolio of the seed.

Psychic guidance reveals the path

When you have planted the seedlings of reality in your psychic portfolio of consciousness, do not worry about *how* they will mature into a full, rich harvest in your life. That is God's secret. As the law works in nature, so it will also work in your own life, constantly raising your own levels of psychic awareness, and guiding you to bring the dreams you have placed in your psychic portfolio into glorious fulfillment.

A PROGRAM TO INCREASE YOUR LEVEL OF PSYCHIC AWARENESS

1. You must consciously build your inner psychic portfolio by selecting the things that you want your higher

psychic mind to materialize for you. Choose the events, persons, conditions and material objects that you would like to have in your life. These conscious choices will have psychic overtones, for you can only externalize in your life that which you have placed in your consciousness. Just as the seed must be placed in the ground before you can produce a crop, so too, the psychic seed must be planted in the soil of consciousness before it can produce the crop of abundance you desire in your life.

Do not be afraid to ask for too much, for this higher psychic mind knows how to achieve any goal you set for yourself.

Have faith that your psychic guidance can lead you to fulfillment of any dream or desire.

Concentrate all the powers of your psychic vision on the things that you ask for.

How a woman's desire for her son materialized

A woman in my lecture group in Carnegie Hall one day told me how she dreamed that her son might become a famous concert pianist. He was only six years of age at that time, but he seemed talented and kept time to music on the radio. This mother had wanted to be a musician when young but her parents couldn't afford piano lessons. Now she was too poor to pay for piano lessons and had no money with which to buy even a second-hand piano. Also, it was during the Second World War and pianos were virtually impossible to get, even if one had the money.

After hearing her seemingly unsolvable problem I told this woman how to create the psychic inner dream and give it to the higher, Cosmic Mind by placing it in the psychic portfolio of the universe. I told her to sit in psychic reverie and visualize a piano in the corner of her living room, and to mentally see her son sitting before the piano, practicing daily. I told her to keep up this daily psychic reverie until the event actually occurred just as she visualized it.

She had faithfully followed my instructions for two

weeks, when she sought me out, her face wreathed in smiles. She said triumphantly, "It worked, exactly as you said it would! I sat every day for an hour and meditated. I visualized the piano, the size, shape and color, in my living room. I even cleared a place for it in one corner, near a fireplace. I told my son to sit and visualize it with me. Then just the other day my phone rang and a friend called me saying she and her husband were moving to a smaller apartment and could not take their upright piano with them. She told me I could have it if I would pay the cost of moving it. Now that piano is in the corner of my living room exactly as I projected it in my mind, and my son is taking his first piano lesson today and is on his way to becoming a concert pianist."

It is true that you can create a dream in this inner psychic portfolio, which is given to the great Cosmic Mind of the universe, and it will be fulfilled in every respect, just as you visualize it.

2. When you go into psychic reverie to obtain information or ask for guidance with your problems, remember that you must try not to depend on *your conscious mind* for solutions or answers. There is a vast intelligence in the universe, which works under psychic vibrations; this is the Cosmic Mind. It has in its storehouse of memory all knowledge, and knows the location of all persons, things and combinations of chemicals and other elements with which it created the universe and all therein. This is a kind of atomic radiation, which is electrical and magnetic in nature, like our present magnetic recording tape. You know how they now record sights and sounds, even color on this recording tape and play it back instantaneously. Everything that happened before the sensitive eye of that recording device has been transmitted to electrical and magnetic pulsations which can be reproduced perfectly in a play-back machine.

The great psychic and Cosmic Mind of the universe is much more sensitive and powerful than any man-made recording device. It has in its universal storehouse of memory everything that has ever occurred in this universe, for it was responsible for its creation. Therefore, when you wish to materialize some object, or create some situation, or find something you've lost, turn with implicit faith to this inner, psychic power.

How to find lost objects through this power

When you lose an object and make frantic efforts to find it, turn to this higher, Cosmic Intelligence and ask it to locate it for you. Sit quietly and say to yourself: Nothing is ever lost to Infinite and Cosmic Mind. It knows the location of my ring. I shall now appeal to this Cosmic Intelligence, confident that I shall be led to where it is.

When you have made this statement to your higher psychic mind, *let go of it* for the moment and go about your ordinary daily activities. You will generally be guided to finding it in a few hours' time at the most.

How valuable lost articles were found

One man had mislaid a valuable paper in his office. He searched everywhere for it and grew more and more excited and confused until he remembered having heard me say at a lecture that nothing is ever lost to Cosmic Mind. So he went into psychic silence and turned the lost paper over to this higher Mind. When he went into the office the next morning he searched the upper right drawer, where he had looked half a dozen times before, and there was the lost paper!

A woman of my lecture group lost a valuable diamond brooch and could not remember where she had lost it. It might have been in a cab on a shopping trip to the city, or in one of the many department stores she had visited that day. She went into psychic reverie and asked the Cosmic Mind to locate the lost object. Then she went to bed that night and forgot about it. During the night she had a dream that the brooch was being held at a certain department store in the lost and found department. She got up the next morning, went to the department store and asked if they had found her brooch. They had, and upon identifying it and proving her own identity, she was given her diamond brooch.

3. In order to increase your level of psychic awareness you must first learn how to build more strongly the power of your five senses; the sense of sight, hearing, touch, smell, and taste. As psychic awareness comes through a subtle sixth sense, using the channels of your sense perception, it is important that you sharpen these five senses so you will have a high degree of sensitivity in your higher brain centers.

In regular practice sessions sit and concentrate on each of your five senses in turn, until you feel they are as sharply attuned as you can possibly make them. Concentrate on listening to strains of music on a phonograph, trying to pick out each instrument in the orchestra. This will help sharpen your sense of hearing.

Look at some object such as a rose, and try to see everything about that rose in crystal-clear vision. Then train your sense of sight by looking out of the window and registering as many objects as possible in one glance.

Develop your sense of touch by feeling various materials with your eyes closed; a piece of wood, silk, cotton, metal—and identify the object and be aware of the subtle differences in each.

Sharpen your sense of taste by practicing with a drop of lemon juice on your tongue, a touch of salt or sugar; something bitter, something sweet, until your sense of taste is highly sensitized.

Smell some fragrance like perfume or incense, or the petals of a flower, until your sense of smell is highly developed.

4. Now carry this development of your five senses a step further; sit in psychic reverie for a day or two, for at least an hour each time, and concentrate on the face of some person who is closely related to you, even if this person is at a distance. Ask him some questions, and then wait for the psychic response of that person's mind. He may not be receiving the thought you project at that exact moment, but the answer will come from the *higher Cosmic Mind which incorporates all persons in its universal intelligence.* This Cosmic Mind can give you an

answer that reflects the person's true psychic response. Then, sometimes you can carry out a question and answer session with some distant person, and let the psychic responses come through at a later time. This is called delayed psychic reaction and may come through in a dream, where you will find yourself holding a conversation with the person, or it may come in fragments of ideas that appear to be the answers to your questions or responses to your conversation.

5. Take some specific problem into your psychic reverie in order to develop this higher psychic mind, and let your mind concentrate on this specific problem, waiting for guidance. The answer might come through in that session or you might be given nothing definite. Then go about your daily affairs, having confidence that the answer will come in a psychic vision, a dream, or an act of guidance where you will be directly led to the place where your solution lies.

6. Sometimes this higher psychic mind will guide you to a channel that you least expect for the solution to your problem. You should not try to choose the channel of your psychic answer, but merely give the problem to your higher psychic mind, and in turn it will be transmitted to the universal psychic clearing house of *Cosmic Mind,* which knows all, sees all and IS *all* things. If you turn to this psychic mind and meditate daily for a half hour or more on any trying or difficult problem that burdens you, then go about your daily activities, you will find that this higher, Cosmic Mind is *already working out a solution to your problem.* All you need do is wait, have patience, have faith, and prepare to receive your good.

How a woman found hidden treasures in Arizona

A woman I know, who used this psychic principle, wanted to discover hidden treasures, such as a gold mine or a diamond field or oil wells. She put this thought into her psychic portfolio and expectantly awaited results, but they did not come—at least, not in the way she had expected. Then one day she got a letter from a friend who lived in Phoenix, Arizona, telling her of the wonderful opportunities in that beautiful state. This woman had a chronic bronchial and sinus condition from the cold in New York City, so she decided to go visit her friend in Phoenix to see if the climate would benefit her. She made the trip, fell in love with the wide open spaces and the beauty of the desert country, found a job there, and soon was urged by her friend to buy land in the area surrounding Phoenix. She bought some acreage and forgot it, but her higher psychic matrix had already been imprinted with *finding hidden treasures,* and never stopped working to make this dream a reality. Within a few years' time business expansion in Phoenix reached out into the suburbs, where this woman owned land. A big chain of gas stations wanted to buy her property, and she sold it to them for a fortune! It was only then that this woman realized she had indeed *found hidden treasures,* as she had instructed her higher psychic centers months before.

7. To increase your level of psychic awareness first increase your soul perception so that you may better receive higher psychic guidance.

Soul perception deals with man's inner awareness of different states of consciousness. It deals with your emotions, your reception of impulses from the higher, Cosmic Mind, which speaks to your soul in the language of vibration. When you stand at the ocean's edge and look out at a magnificent sunset, you vibrate to the universal cosmic image of divine beauty, color, harmony and joy. Your spirits are elevated and your mind soars into lofty realms of divine inspiration and beauty. This is soul perception.

8. To help increase your level of psychic awareness on different planes of consciousness, use the following questionnaire or make up similar questions that fit your own life, to stir into action the psychic centers of your higher consciousness. The answers to these questions may come through in one psychic session or it may take several days or even weeks to achieve the fulfillment of all your requests. Then too, some of the psychic guidance may come through unexpected channels where you receive a letter or phone call from some person who is the connecting link to your solution. It may come through the acci-

dental meeting of some person who is alerted by the Cosmic Mind to serve as a channel for fulfillment of your desires.

QUESTIONS TO INCREASE YOUR LEVEL OF PSYCHIC AWARENESS

a. What goals should I try to achieve in my future?

b. What are my natural talents and abilities?

c. What steps should I take to achieve these goals?

d. How can I create a more dynamic personality and be magnetic and popular?

e. What are my outstanding defects and how can I change them into positive personality traits?

f. What is the purpose of my life and how can I best fulfill that destiny for which I was born?

g. What should my life work be and how can I get into it?

h. How and where can I attract people into my life who will prove helpful and constructive in achieving my life goal?

i. What steps can I take that will lead me to acquire wealth and abundance?

j. How can I solve my personal problems and achieve peace, tranquility and happiness?

k. How can I develop the creative gifts of writing, painting, acting, singing, inventing, composing (or any other gift on which you wish psychic guidance)?

When you have made out this questionnaire and have gone into psychic reverie for at least an hour a day for some weeks, you should have enough psychic awareness developed so you can receive direct communication with your higher psychic mind centers.

When you have completed this phase of psychic awareness, you should then put into the psychic portfolio of this higher mind the PSYCHIC BLUEPRINT FOR YOUR FUTURE.

Write out a complete list of your inner desires, hopes, and aspirations that you would like to materialize in your present or future life. This psychic blueprint will act as a guide to Cosmic Intelligence in providing from its storehouse of abundance all the conditions that you require for the fulfillment of your destiny.

Write on a sheet of paper the following words:

My Psychic Blueprint for Future Fulfillment

Then list on that sheet the following desires, or those that you personally wish to materialize in your own life. Write these out in your own handwriting, for there is some psychic power stirred into action through the kinetic sense of writing things down. Following are some typical situations:

1. I want a change in my work. I desire work as a . . . (here list the type of work you would like to be in; such as accounting, nurse's aide, teacher, dental technician, designer, artist, actor, etc). Guide me to the right place where I can be trained to do this type of work.

2. I would like to be in a business of my own. (Here name the business; restaurant, flower shop, decorating business, etc.) Guide me to take the right steps to become independent in this business.

3. I would like to develop creative gifts and talents so I can release my imagination in channels of beauty and creative good. (Here state what creative gift you would like, such as writing, painting, music, designing, or cosmotology.)

4. I would like to have enough money to meet my current bills and to give me a great degree of security in the future. For present needs I would like to be guided to attracting the sum of $1,000 and for future security I would like to have $100,000 or more.

5. I would like psychic guidance for attracting my true soul mate in love and marriage. I desire the following traits of character and mental qualities in my future mate. I would like her to be honest, good, pleasant and cheerful, sympathetic and understanding, and of high moral character.

6. I would like to be able to travel to different coun-

tries and would appreciate psychic guidance as to how I can accomplish this on my present income.

7. I would like to receive psychic guidance on how I may obtain a beautiful home in which to rear my future family and build my life. I would like to live in . . . (name the city or location, such as country, suburbs of New York), and I would like the house to be . . . (here describe the type of home you want, size, number of rooms, one- or two-storied, etc.).

8. I would like to be guided in building my social life with people who are important and who may be able to help me achieve a better standard of living and higher goals.

When you have completed this psychic blueprint, read it over every morning upon arising, and every night, just before retiring. This method of filling your psychic portfolio with the ideas, images, objects, and situations you would like to have in your life, is one that has worked miracles in the lives of thousands who have used it. Not only does it help raise the level of your own psychic awareness, but it brings into focus in your own psychic portfolio of inner dreams, all the psychic thought forms which will be communicated to the Cosmic Mind of the universe, which will fulfill them for you in its own mysterious fashion in the fourth-dimensional world of spirit.

Summary of Chapter 12

1. How to create the psychic portfolio within the consciousness where psychic awareness begins.
2. How psychic guidance can be invoked for achieving the things you desire in your future.
3. The regime for increasing psychic awareness.
4. Desire, faith, and concentration—three keys to psychic awareness.
5. How one woman used this secret to materialize a piano and lessons for her son.
6. How you may tap the cosmic storehouse of memory for anything that you desire and cause it to release psychic guidance.

7. How you can find lost objects through this power.
8. How you can build psychic awareness by concentrating on the five senses first and raising your sense of psychic awareness.
9. How you can use psychic reverie to solve problems.
10. Soul perception which will give you greater psychic awareness and help you in your future life.
11. How to raise your level of psychic awareness through meditating on specific questions in the psychic silence.
12. How you can create your psychic blueprint of destiny and bring into your psychic portfolio all the dreams and aspirations that you have for your future.

chapter 13

The Dynamic Laws Available for Developing Your Hidden Psychic Powers

You can develop psychic powers, intuition and the gift of clairvoyance, with a little practice. Everyone is psychic to a certain extent.

Have you ever thought of a person and then had the telephone ring, and the person you thought of was calling you?

Have you ever had a dream in which some event occurred which was a preview of something that happened later in your life?

Have you felt a hunch not to do a certain thing, and then later found out that your hunch was correct?

These are proofs that on occasion you are using the higher dimensions of your mind where the true psychic and clairvoyant gift resides. You can develop this power like any other mental gift.

HOW LAWS OF PSYCHIC PHENOMENA WORK IN NATURE

The laws of psychic phenomena work as definitely as the laws which control gravity, electricity and magnetism. Psychic powers, intuition and clairvoyance are a part of the human consciousness and are natural, not supernatural. The reason why more people do not function on this plane of extrasensory perception is because they have ignored the intuitive and psychic impulses of their higher minds so long that they are no longer sensitive to their subtle promptings.

When a child accidentally touches a hot stove he does not stop and reason, "I must withdraw my hand so I will not be burned." Some inner *compulsion* causes him to pull his hand back without questioning why.

The intelligence which causes a person to intuitively do something to preserve his life issues from a higher mind center than the conscious brain. We term this higher power psychic or "intuitive."

When this intuition comes in the form of a mental image, such as an imaginative picture that flashes on the screen of the higher consciousness, we call this prompting clairvoyant. If there are accompanying words with this mental picture, and they come silently or audibly, we call this form of extrasensory perception clairaudient.

These forms of mental and psychic guidance operate under definite cosmic laws, and when you once understand these laws you can tap this higher intuitive power and be guided, protected, informed, educated and in other ways motivated to shape your destiny with a maximum degree of safety and wisdom.

We cannot explain why some people receive these accurate visions and others do not, but I have known hundreds of such cases where people have been warned of impending disaster. When they listened to the psychic voice within or observed the warning of the clairvoyant vision, they were spared, while others succumbed.

A CLAIRVOYANT VISION
HER SISTER WOULD HAVE TWINS

Do psychic and clairvoyant visions come only as warnings of disaster or death? No, there are many other psychic visions which people receive that are not as spectacular and dramatic. We seldom hear of these, for they are minor in nature and concern only trivial, everyday happenings. These psychic promptings and visions can concern such matters as a change in jobs, or an impulse to move to another location, or the impending visit of a friend or relative who has been away for years. Sometimes these clairvoyant visions show a person receiving a large sum of money through the settling of a will. One instance I know of concerned a psychic vision a woman had that her

169

sister, who was in the first three months of pregnancy, would have twins. Not even the doctors knew this at the time, and sure enough, when the delivery came, this woman had twin sons. She had even predicted they would be boys! Her clairvoyant vision had come to her in psychic reverie while she sat with her eyes wide open thinking about something else.

"Coming events cast their shadows before," the old proverb says. This is literally true regarding psychic and clairvoyant prophecy. There seems to be some great Cosmic Intelligence which knows the shape of events to come. When we are able to get on this cosmic and psychic wavelength, we receive the psychic vision and have a preview of the future.

Sometimes we can tune in on the event before it is to happen, and this is called precognition. Often while the event is occurring we will receive a psychic flash that it is happening.

A PSYCHIC WARNING
THAT A BROTHER HAD DIED

A woman reported a psychic happening to me that her husband witnessed, which was a precognitive flash. They were having breakfast when the mailman brought a letter, which she recognized as being from the city where her brother lived. Before opening the letter she remarked, "My brother George is dead!" Her husband was startled for there had been no discussion about her brother's health and, as far as they knew, he was in good health. Upon reading the letter the woman began to cry, for it carried the news that her brother had indeed had a heart attack three days before and was hospitalized.

Within one hour their phone rang and it was the brother's wife who reported, "George died half an hour ago in the hospital." She had not called them before, to keep them from worrying over the heart attack, but had merely written about it in the letter. This woman had a true psychic vision of the death of her brother at almost the exact time the event occurred over a thousand miles away!

USE THESE 10 DYNAMIC LAWS TO DEVELOP PSYCHIC POWERS, INTUITION AND CLAIRVOYANCY

Law No. 1 Invoke the Law of Self-Preservation to Unlock Psychic Powers

The strongest drive in the human psyche is the will to live. This will expresses itself through the urge of self-preservation.

Something in the higher psychic mind causes you to want to preserve the flame of life, to be healthy, to live as long as you can. When this psychic force is dimmed, the will to die is invoked and we find people overeating, overdrinking, oversmoking and exposing themselves to dangers which threaten their very existence.

You can invoke this dynamic psychic law of self-preservation and receive from your higher psychic centers a flow of intuitive and clairvoyant guidance which will protect you from danger and assure you of living out your natural life span in security and comfort.

To receive the maximum psychic guidance from your higher mind, you can intensify this natural urge of self-preservation.

1. Live with a purpose. Have a reason for living other than to make money and be happy. Have a desire to create something useful and good which you can share with the world.

2. Live to love, as well as love to live. This will give your higher psychic powers an impetus to fan the spark of life and give you vitality, energy and life force to do your life work. Love arouses the higher psychic centers and often releases psychic energy which can overcome many of life's problems.

3. Ask your higher psychic mind for daily guidance in matters of safety and protection for you and your family.

4. Carefully analyze your dreams for you may be

receiving clairvoyant or psychic impressions in your dreams which are warnings of future conditions of danger in your life.

HOW A WARNING OF DANGER
CAME THROUGH PSYCHIC DREAM

A woman received such a psychic clairvoyant dream shortly after her husband had died. She had been forced to move into a large apartment where several older, widowed women had rooms. She put all her things into storage and went into this apartment temporarily until she could find a suitable small apartment.

One night she dreamed that she saw her husband, exactly as he had been in life except that he was smoking a pipe, and he had never smoked anything but cigarettes. She asked him, "Why are you smoking a pipe?"

He replied, "The house is on fire. The house is on fire." This was all he said, and the woman awakened very distressed and not understanding the reason for her dream. She called the storage where her household goods were stored and made sure that her things were insured for fire. Then she forgot about the dream.

A few nights later she awakened from a sound sleep with a feeling of heaviness in her chest, as if she could not breathe. She did not smell smoke but some strange inner compulsion made her reach for the light. It would not turn on! Then she had a definite sense of danger and urgency, and somehow she knew that the apartment house was on fire. She staggered to her feet, and wet a towel which she put over her nose and mouth. She had heard somewhere that this was what one should do in event of fire. She opened her door and rushed out into the dark hallway. She walked a few steps and stumbled over the body of a fireman who had been overcome and was lying there in the hall. She reached the stairs, as the elevator was not operating due to the power failure. She fell down a flight of stairs, stumbling over fire hose and men who were rushing up the stairs. She managed to get down the full seven flights of stairs to the street, and there, in the lobby lying stretched out in a row, were twelve bodies of elderly persons who had died of smoke inhalation!

Law No. 2   Express Your Psychic
Urge to Evolve Your Creative Ego to
a Higher Level of Activity

"Man shall not live by bread alone." You were born to achieve magnificence and ego fulfillment. Unless you use your higher psychic centers to evolve higher and higher in the scale of evolution, you defeat the very purpose of your existence.

You can turn every day to this higher psychic center of your mind and receive guidance regarding your various moves in life.

Remember—you were born to know ego fulfillment. This means the full expression of your nature in creative patterns which bring you happiness, peace and love fulfillment.

Turn to this higher psychic mind and ask it to guide you in this department of your life. Ask it these questions:

How can I achieve my true life goal?
How can I overcome my personal problems and be happy and peaceful?
How can I attract the right friends and acquaintances who will give me the right social life?
How can I release more creative mind power to become inspired to do better work?

A WOMAN IGNORED PSYCHIC WARNING
AND WAS SUED

You can receive psychic impressions about people whom you attract, and ask this higher mind if you should trust them. One woman who did not follow a psychic prompting, lived to regret it. She wanted to go into business with a woman who represented herself as being capable and experienced in the line of business they intended to enter. Something about her struck this other woman as being dishonest, and she went into psychic reverie to ask for instructions. The warnings came through: *Do not trust this woman. She will later sue you.*

Then she saw the sum of one hundred thousand dollars written over this woman's head.

She ignored this psychic warning and went ahead and opened the business with this woman. Three months later the business failed and this woman sued her for exactly one hundred thousand dollars! Of course she did not collect, but it cost the other woman several thousand dollars to defend herself in the court action. If she had listened to this psychic prompting of her higher mind, what grief and expense she could have been saved.

Law No. 3   Stimulate Psychic Vision
Through Your Imagination

The creative imagination is closely allied to psychic powers. The clairvoyant images one receives are channeled through the creative imagination.

Sit in psychic reverie every day to develop this gift of clairvoyance through your higher imagination.

Project yourself to some imaginary scene and ask for information about it. You might choose a home you wish to live in at some future date; or a job you hope to have; or some social function you would like to attend. In your mind's eye live in that dimension of time and space, and let what will come through. Many times you will actually be invoking the power of higher psychic reception, and visions will come through of things that will actually happen to you in the future!

Law No. 4   Release Psychic Energy
Through Your Emotions and by the
Power of Concentration

Psychic and clairvoyant visions depend on the release of psychic energy. You cannot send psychic thought forms or receive them unless you know how to project this psychic energy through your emotions and by the power of concentration.

In your daily psychic sessions you must stimulate your higher psychic centers through holding one or more of these emotions in your consciousness, and then concentrating all the psychic energy you possess on these emotions.

1. The emotion of faith
2. The emotion of love
3. The emotion of good
4. The emotion of unselfishness
5. The emotion of charity
6. The emotion of hope

These six emotions have been found to create psychic excitation of the higher intuitive faculties and help release psychic energy for clairvoyance, clairaudience and psychic vision.

CREATE AND PROJECT PSYCHIC IMAGES THROUGH COSMOGRAPHY

Through a process which I have named *cosmography*, you can create the psychic images in your mind, imbue them with emotion, and then your higher mind will release them to the Cosmic Mind, where they will be made a living reality.

In your psychic reverie practice this process of psychic cosmography and clothe the pictures you form with emotional energy. Then quietly project them to the Cosmic Intelligence and wait for psychic guidance or clairvoyant visions regarding your desire.

For example: You might desire money to help, let us say, educate your children. Money is too vague and indefinite an image, so project psychically the cosmograph of your children going through college and being trained for specific work. Now, in psychic reverie you will involve the emotions of love of your family, a desire to do good for them, the emotion of unselfishness, of charity, of faith that you will accomplish your desire, and of hope for the future good.

As you sit in psychic reverie projecting this cosmograph to the Cosmic Mind, you will see what psychic impulses come through to you.

HOW A WOMAN EDUCATED HER CHILDREN THROUGH CLAIRVOYANT GUIDANCE

A woman who used this type of psychic cosmography to educate her three children and send them all through college, reported to me how she used this psychic power.

She had lost her husband through an accident and had three children—two sons, aged thirteen and sixteen, and one daughter, aged eleven. The insurance money was nearly gone and she was on her own, with no training for a job and unable to leave her children to go out into the world to make a living.

Luckily she had studied these laws of psychic phenomena in my lectures in Hollywood. She lived out in the San Fernando Valley in a home that still had a heavy mortgage on it. She had no one to turn to, and in desperation turned to her higher psychic forces for guidance.

She held the cosmograph of her three children being able to obtain a higher education, of paying off the mortgage on her home and achieving security for their future.

No definite psychic message came through in her first few sessions of psychic reverie, so she went about her activities, with confidence that guidance would come. She was an excellent cook and could bake wonderful pies and cakes. One day when she was walking past a construction job near her home, she saw the men lounging around eating cold lunches at noon. A psychic flash suddenly came through to her: *Take warm lunches to these men, featuring your pies and cakes.* She followed this psychic hunch and began to visit building sites nearby, taking warm foods, coffee in thermos jugs and her tasty pies and cakes. The men were delighted to be able to buy such delicious, warm food, and soon she had more business than she could take care of. She took the last of her insurance money and made a down payment on a small panel truck. She loaded it with her sandwiches and other foods, and visited several building sites where the men flocked to buy her appetizing foods. When summer came, her oldest son drove the truck for her, and soon she bought another truck, which she drove, and they were visiting building sites several miles around in the Valley and in Los Angeles, selling everything she could cook.

Before another year had passed this woman, through her psychic guidance, added another truck to her fleet and was making so much money that she was able to pay all expenses, keep her home, educate her children and build security for the future.

Now, the psychic answer to your problems may be totally different from this woman's, but if you build your psychic cosmographs and project them to Cosmic Mind, you will be psychically guided to the solution of your problems.

Law No. 5   Create Spiritual
Magnetism to Link You with the
Cosmic Clearing House of all
Psychic Communication

The law of spiritual magnetism states: You attract that which you hold in consciousness and magnetize.

If you wish to use psychic and clairvoyant power and receive thought forms, visions, psychic guidance, you must first magnetize the psychic filaments of your mind by passing through them the impressions, persons, situations and events that you wish to receive through clairvoyance.

Put into the psychic filaments of your consciousness these magnetic thoughts to link you with Cosmic Mind:

1.   I desire help in my business so I can make more money.

2.   I wish to magnetize friends and acquaintances so I can lead a better social life.

3.   I wish psychic guidance to a better job where I can have a bigger income.

4.   I wish psychic guidance on problems of health; how to be stronger, healthier and live longer.

177

5. I wish to magnetize and attract happiness, the right marriage partner, and fulfillment in love.

6. I magnetize a home of my own and wish psychic guidance as to how I can go about finding the right place in which to live.

7. I wish psychic guidance as to how I can solve my problems and find inner peace and contentment.

Remember—the Cosmic Mind knows *your right place in life,* knows how to make you successful and rich; knows how to guide you to your right destiny.

Sometimes when you magnetize the image of money and project it to the Cosmic Mind, it comes to you in such a mysterious fashion that you can hardly believe it. You will attract to yourself the psychic images that you magnetize on the wavelength that fits your particular needs and your character.

HOW MONEY WAS MAGNETIZED
THROUGH PSYCHIC PROJECTION

A strange instance of how magnetizing money can often lead to its acquisition was related to me by a very close friend. He seldom went to the race track, but one day he went with friends, and before the races began, he was at the bar. He overheard a man order a drink by the name of "seven and seven." He had no idea that it was a brand of whisky in a popular beverage having the number seven in the name. But his higher psychic centers clicked at the words seven and seven, and he told his friends, "I am going to play seven and seven in the daily double." They laughed at his childish faith in a casual remark he'd overheard and they bet other numbers.

The first horse that came in was number seven! Then they all waited anxiously for the running of the second race. In the stretch, number seven didn't seem to have a chance, but just then the number one horse stumbled and lost his pace, and number seven came in to win.

What do you think this daily double paid? Seven hundred and seventy-seven dollars! To my friend this was too much to expect of coincidence and he felt certain he had received psychic guidance. It was almost as if Cosmic Mind, with a great sense of humor, decided to bring about one of those impossible combinations of events which defy all reason and logic.

Law No. 6   Elevate Your Conscious-
ness from the Third-Dimensional
World of Matter to the Fourth-
Dimensional World of Thought and
Spirit

Psychic phenomena work in the fourth-dimensional world of thought and spirit. Soul is not imprisoned by matter but is able to rise above the limitations of the flesh and have experiences in another dimension of time and space.

When you go into psychic reverie and try to receive psychic guidance or clairvoyant visions, remember that you must free yourself from the chains of matter and substance. You must rise into the psychic stratosphere of pure spirit.

Remove your mind from problems, money matters, people and things, and elevate your consciousness into the realm of the absolute. Meditate in the psychic silence on:

1.   Absolute Power
2.   Absolute Intelligence
3.   Absolute Good
4.   Absolute Beauty
5.   Absolute Joy

Now align your psychic self with your total concept of cosmic power—the universe and all therein, with its mysterious flow of dynamic energy from the sun and from the stars in space.

Now align yourself with Cosmic Intelligence, and see all the evidences of this intelligence in everything in nature.

Now align yourself with all good, all beauty, all joy, and feel the transcendental radiatory power that flows into your psychic centers of mind and soul, through the cosmic spirit.

Law No. 7   Use the Law of Psychic
Fusion of Your Soul with the Soul of
the Universe

Your soul is the true receiver of psychic pulsations
from the soul of the universe. Your mind is only the channel which interprets these higher pyschic and clairvoyant
pulsations.

In order to achieve clearer psychic reception, or to be
able to send psychic messages to the souls of others, it is
necessary that you achieve soul-fusion with the universal
soul. This can only be done when your motives are pure
and high and unselfish.

When you go into psychic reverie set the stage by having
a peaceful, quiet environment. Light a candle and have it
burning as you concentrate on receiving psychic impulses.
Have some incense burning and soft music playing. By
putting yourself into a state of psychic receptivity, you will
help stimulate the neuropsychic centers of your consciousness and will receive much better psychic vision.

PSYCHIC POWER IS THE UNIVERSAL
LANGUAGE OF THE SOUL

There is a universal language of music, which speaks to
all souls alike. There is also a universal language of the
soul, and its cosmic vibrations speak to all humanity in
the rhythm of the seasons, in the silent growth within the
soil, in the fulfillment of nature's elements. The language of
the Cosmic Soul speaks to man through universal love.

When you want to achieve this fusion of your soul with
the Cosmic Soul of the universe, elevate your consciousness to the highest, most noble and unselfish plane of action that you can visualize. Love humanity and have a
desire to serve it with your psychic gifts; love God and
have a desire to serve Him and praise Him for the blessings He has showered upon you. Use the key forces of
faith, love and prayer to unlock the universal storehouse
of psychic and clairvoyant gifts which exist in the vast soul
of the universe.

Law No. 8   The Dynamics of
Psychokinesis

You can use the law of psycho-dynamics to mold and
shape matter with the power of mind and spirit, through a
process known as psychokinesis.

Science has now determined that mental and spiritual
energy may be used to influence and shape material substance. All creation is made up of pinpoints of psychic and
spiritual energy, which manifest themselves in different
forms of creation. What you see as solid substance is in
reality nothing but a vibrating mass of atoms being held
together by the invisible law of centrifugal and centripetal
motion—meaning atoms flying out from a common center, and atoms whirling towards and held to a center or
core. All creation follows this cosmic law.

You can set up a centrifugal psychic center, in which
you bombard the atmosphere with the atomic energy of
your mind, or you can become a psychic center of centripetal action, which will assure you of receiving the
thoughts, clairvoyant visions and impressions in the psychic
center of your being, that are being projected from other
minds to the Cosmic Mind of the universe.

HOW A BABY'S LIFE WAS SAVED
THROUGH PSYCHO-DYNAMICS

Psycho-dynamics concerns the force and emotional
charge with which you color your thoughts. If you want to
reach another person you must send emotionalized thought
forms, such as one woman did, who was baby-sitting with
a two-year-old child. She knew that the mother and father
were going to the theater in New York City, but she
couldn't for the life of her remember which theater. The
baby became ill during the evening, had a fever and was in
great distress. The baby-sitter had some experience in psychic phenomena, and she sent out an emotional distress
signal to the mother: "Call your house at once, your baby
is very sick! Call your house immediately, your baby is
sick!" She kept this psychic SOS up for at least half an

hour, when suddenly the phone rang, and the agitated voice of the mother said, "I had an urge to call home. Is the baby all right?" The baby sitter told her of the child's illness and the parents rushed home immediately, and called a doctor. The child recovered completely, but the baby-sitter knew that she had made a telepathic contact with the child's mother.

PSYCHIC ENERGY CAN MOVE PHYSICAL OBJECTS

Scientists have proved conclusively that mind and spirit can motivate matter. Dr. Rhine, of Duke University proved this. There are thousands of authenticated cases where people have exerted a psychic influence on bodies, objects and environments.

A child in one family had this psychic power of psychokinesis to such an extent that when he was in a room objects would go flying off the mantle, pictures would fall off the wall and vases and plaster objects would break for no apparent reason.

Many times this form of psychic energy released through psychokinesis is thought to emanate from departed spirits and this is known as a poltergeist. However, it has been discovered that a person who possesses a superabundance of this spiritual and psychic energy, through psycho-dynamics, can release a power that definitely affects people and material objects.

To develop this power of generating psychic and spiritual energy, it is necessary that you practice projecting the stream of psychic energy at some person or some object, with the intent of motivating its atomic and molecular structure. It is better to begin with a person, and project a radiant stream of psychic energy to his psychic centers, urging him to phone you, write you, or meet you on the street. Then practice projecting thought forms to some person on a particular subject and check later to see if he received your messages.

You can also practice by rolling dice and seeing if they will turn up as you mentally project them; for instance, concentrate on seven, or eleven or any other number. I knew one man who tried this experiment at Las Vegas and projected the number eleven, and he threw eleven three consecutive times to win a handsome sum of money.

Law No. 9 Use Psychic Replay to Review the Past and to Project Future Events Through the Process of Precognition and Retro-cognition

Precognition relates to a preview of the future through the psychic faculties, by tapping the Cosmic Mind and projecting that which is about to happen.

Retro-cognition concerns the replaying of past psychic events in history or from the minds of other people, and living in the knowledge, inspiration and fulfillment of these past historic events.

When using the higher psychic mind for precognition, you should go into the silence and hold your mind still. Visualize the screen of your mind, like a television or movie screen. Mentally see the Cosmic Mind like a giant projector out in time and space, focusing upon the screen of your higher psychic centers the thought forms, pictures, scenes and events that you are calling up in psychic reverie.

HOW TO REPLAY PAST EVENTS THROUGH RETRO-COGNITION

Very often you may want to project yourself backwards in time and space and replay cosmic and psychic images of past historic events or thought forms from the minds of great geniuses who have lived in the past. Remember, all thought forms, all sounds, voices and impulses from the minds of others are still in existence in the magnetic and electrical layers of the cosmos.

Scientists now say that if they could build a big enough amplifier, they could play back the voice of Christ giving his Sermon on the Mount; Abraham Lincoln's Gettysburg Address, and Washington's first inaugural address. If we could replay the cosmic sound track of the universe we could pick up the sounds and sights that occurred in history, just as a video tape machine used in television now, can record sounds and pictures, and replay them instantly.

The higher psychic centers are more flexible than a machine. The human consciousness, when it is once trained, can tap this cosmic sound track of the universe and pick up with the sensitive antenna of the higher mind, the sights and sounds that made up the pageant of history and through retro-cognition, replay them on the screen of the psychic centers.

Law No. 10   Elevation of Your
Consciousness to the Cosmo-Psychic
Realm

Express the soul urge to find cosmic fulfillment as the ultimate spiritual goal in this world.

When you elevate the consciousness to the cosmic realm, you will be able to project the psychic images of true infinite beauty, infinite goodness, infinite truth, infinite love and infinite joy.

When you sit in psychic reverie for this last great psychic law, concentrate on the highest ideals of spiritual beauty that you can visualize. The Cosmic Mind will flood your higher psychic nerve centers with lofty inspiration and noble thoughts, if you can raise the rate of vibration of your soul to that of the cosmic level.

Concentrate in turn on each of the infinite forces given above; hold the image of infinite beauty in your consciousness, and see what comes through. Stimulate your psychic centers by looking at the beauty of flowers and trees and the myriad forms of natural beauty that surround you.

Practice expressing the force of infinite goodness, and you will stimulate your psychic centers to project good automatically in your life.

Summary of Chapter 13

1. The laws of psychic phenomena, as definite as the laws controlling gravity, magnetism and electricity.
2. Clairvoyant and clairaudient visions often coming as dreams.
3. The ten dynamic laws to develop psychic powers.
4. Psychic centers stimulated by the will to live.
5. Psychic powers unlocked through evolving the creative ego.
6. How to stimulate psychic and clairvoyant vision through imagination.
7. How to use concentration to release psychic energy through the emotions.
8. How you can create psychic and spiritual magnetism to link you with the cosmic clearing house of psychic communication.
9. How to create psychic fusion of your soul with the soul of the universe.
10. How to use the law of psychokinesis to influence persons and objects, and motivate conditions in your future.
11. How to use psychic replay for process of precognition to predict your future, and retro-cognition to project into the past.
12. How you can express the soul urge to find cosmic fulfillment and increase your psychic and clairvoyant powers.

chapter 14

How to Perform
Living Miracles by Using the
Psychic Matrix of the Universe

You can truly become a miracle worker when you learn the secret that Cosmic Mind uses to create all things in the universe.

You can change your physical body, creating a pattern of health, vitality, youth and energy through this principle of the psychic matrix.

You can create an image of money, cars, houses, land, stocks and bonds—and the psychic matrix of the universe will set to work to evolve them for you under its universal laws.

You can attract people, love, fulfillment, happiness, abundance—all these treasures are waiting for you in the psychic matrix of the universe—when you know how to invoke this tremendous psychic power.

THE INVISIBLE CREATIVE PATTERN OF LIFE

There is an invisible psychic matrix or mold which exists in the secret interstices of the universe. When Cosmic Intelligence wants to create anything from stars to human beings, it pours invisible, creative substance made up of atoms and molecules, into this psychic matrix and it produces the object that is desired.

For example, the matrix of an orange is contained in its seed. If you cut open that seed and examine it carefully, you cannot find any visible evidence of a tree, leaves, fragrant blossoms or the final edible fruit that will issue from that vibratory psychic matrix of the orange seed.

The creative miracle of all the universe is involved in this principle of the invisible psychic matrix of the cosmos.

The matrix of the baby chick that is to be born is in the invisible germ within the fertilized egg. There is no resemblance whatever between the egg and the finished product that will break out of that shell in twenty-one days' time. Truly this is a cosmic miracle.

HOW YOU MAY CREATE YOUR OWN PSYCHIC MATRIX

You may create your own psychic matrix and learn how to mold and shape anything you want to have in your life, in structuring psychic images and thought forms. You can then project these psychic images to the cosmic matrix, and under the laws of invisible atomic power you can create living miracles.

Into the invisible psychic matrix which you create in your consciousness, Cosmic Intelligence will pour the invisible spiritual protoplasm to create anything that you imagine.

To illustrate how this creative miracle works, let us see how a sculptor uses this principle of the matrix or mold. The sculptor has a mental image of a figure he wants to create. He imprints this mental image from his psychic centers, to a malleable substance, such as clay. Then when this image is fixed in clay he may want to reproduce it in something more permanent, such as bronze, or plaster. He makes a mold around his original clay figure of either plaster or moulage, a kind of rubberized material. This mold or matrix duplicates perfectly the original figure in every detail. From this matrix or mold one may create thousands of identical figures.

YOU MAY PROJECT ANYTHING YOU WISH IN YOUR PSYCHIC MATRIX

You may project anything you wish in your psychic matrix if you use this cosmic secret for creating new forms and patterns.

All forms of creation exist in the psychic matrix of the

cosmos as vibrations or invisible pulsations. The vibration that creates a delicate snowflake is vastly different from that which shapes a pink or white rose, yet the principle of its creation is similar.

One scientist in France studied snowflakes over a period of forty years and discovered one of nature's hidden secrets: no two snowflakes that he examined under a microscope were ever alike!

PROGRAM FOR USING THE PSYCHIC MATRIX TO PERFORM LIVING MIRACLES IN YOUR LIFE

To tap the miracle life force in the matrix of the Cosmic Mind and channel it to your body for perfect health, youth and vitality, take these simple steps:

1. Sit in the psychic silence and concentrate all the power of your mind on the psychic centers of your brain. Visualize a golden flame rising from the base of your spine to your brain, and then gushing, like a fountain of liquid flame over the entire surface of the brain, stimulating the psychic centers of the pineal gland, in the very center of your brain.

2. As you hold this concentration on the golden flame, breathe deeply ten times, holding your breath to the count of four, then releasing it on the count of four. As you do this create the psychic matrix of *a perfect body,* by saying aloud or to yourself: "I now tap the psychic centers of my consciousness and form the perfect matrix of a healthy, strong, youthful body. Psychic energy now flows from the dynamic centers of my being, and floods every atom and cell of my brain and body with *life—life—life.*"

3. You can repeat this dynamic psychic statement at least four times, all the while breathing slowly and deeply. Then concentrate a moment on the golden flame of the sun in your mind. Now say to your higher psychic mind: "I now tap the golden life energy of the cosmic sun that is the psychic matrix for creating all life and all energy in the universe. I now flood my being with this golden light of youth, vitality and eternal energy. I am one with cosmic light and life and truth, and my body now reflects the

strength and energy of the flaming spiritual sun which gives the cosmos birth."

4. Whenever you walk on the streets or about your home, adopt the cosmic rhythm of graceful motion and vitality. Keep the head erect, the spine straight, the breathing deep and slow and rhythmic; this is the posture of youth and life. When you slouch or shuffle as you walk, you create the psychic matrix of age and infirmity and your psychic centers are stifled in their flow of youth, vitality, energy and health to your body cells.

HOW TO SET YOU PSYCHIC AND BIOLOGICAL TIMECLOCK IN THE PSYCHIC MATRIX OF HEALTH AND YOUTH

There is a psychic and biological timeclock which you may set in your psychic centers in the pattern of youth and health. This biological timeclock can be seen in nature when it tells a caterpillar the time to break out of its cocoon and become a butterfly, or in the various elements of nature which tell the seed when to sprout and grow into a harvest. This biological timeclock is in the seasons, telling us when it is spring, summer, fall and winter. It is in the flow of the tides, and in the life cycles of all living creatures. Scientists now find that they can change this biological timeclock for some creatures causing them to lose their cosmic rhythm and become confused in their various life cycles.

To set your psychic and biological timeclock in the psychic matrix of youth and health and long life, give your higher psychic mind instructions as follows: "I now set my psychic and biological timeclock in the matrix of perfection and ultimate growth to achieve my true life destiny. I reflect universal order, harmony and rhythm in the cosmic life force that keeps my body healthy and causes my cells to be nourished with the right elements, bringing me to the fulfillment of my cosmic destiny."

To create the matrix in your consciousness for new patterns of creativity in business, finance and investments, and become as rich as you wish to be, take these steps:

1. Go into the creative, psychic silence, holding in your consciousness the definite steps you wish to take and which you wish psychic guidance about.

2. When you begin to create the psychic matrix of security and financial stability, you can give your higher psychic centers instructions as follows, or make up your own statements, to fit your particular business and financial needs:

I now instruct my higher psychic centers to create the matrix of business and financial success for my future. I draw upon the Cosmic Memory bank and ask it to send through creative patterns of action, ideas, and programs that will help me sell my products, make the right contacts, and find the most fruitful channels through which I may express my creative talents.

How one man attracted $20,000 through the psychic matrix

A man worked for an advertising agency, but he needed more money and advancement, which did not seem to come easily. He began to create the psychic matrix and asked for ten thousand dollars cash. To stimulate the psychic image of what ten thousand dollars was like, I told him to go to the Money Museum of the Chase Manhattan Bank at 50th Street and the Avenue of the Americas, where they have a ten thousand dollar bill on exhibit in a glass case. This man was told to concentrate on that ten thousand dollar bill, to photograph it mentally in the psychic matrix of his mind; and to begin to work mentally to attract that sum of money or more, in the near future.

This man did this exercise in concentration several times, and daily worked with creating the psychic matrix, and in two months' time he got an idea for a television commercial that brought him a ten thousand dollar bonus! From this he went on to other successes, won another ten thousand dollar bonus and in one year's time, opened his own advertising agency and soon had twenty-five million dollars worth of advertising contracts for television, magazines and newspapers!

3. Build the mental and psychic equivalent of money in your psychic matrix. Money in itself is of no use. You cannot eat or drink money, as such. However, the psychic equivalents of money are many; rent, food, clothing, luxuries, travel, beautiful furnishings, automobiles, cultural benefits, and security—these are the psychic equivalents of money. In your psychic matrix create these equivalents by affirming them and building their prototype in your higher psychic brain centers.

I am now a center of psychic power and energy, creating a whirlpool of spiritual and mental activity which will magnetize money and its equivalents into my orbit. I create the psychic matrix for the equivalents of money. I desire a home, beautiful furnishings, an automobile, travel, jewelry, nourishing food, fine clothes, cultural benefits and all the security and luxury that go with success and riches. I project the psychic energy in the matrix of the cosmos which can create these benefits for my loved ones and myself.

To create the psychic matrix for solving daily problems, motivating people, changing your environment and other purposes, use these techniques:

Go into the psychic silence and choose the persons you wish to motivate. Either have a photograph of them, or hold their faces, one at a time, in the forefront of your consciousness. Then concentrate a stream of radiant psychic energy to their minds by calling out their names, and stating the action which you wish them to perform. We will take someone named John for an example:

John, I am sending out thoughts to motivate your actions for your good and for mine. You will give me the advancement in my job that I desire. You will see how hard I work, and that I am worth more money. I am helping your firm with my services, and you will

191

recognize that I deserve this advancement to a better job. I project the psychic thought forms now that will create in the matrix of your consciousness the action that I desire and deserve.

You can solve your daily problems, using this psychic technique, as well as the method given elsewhere in this book to handle most problems.

Go into the psychic silence and write down the problem which you wish to have dissolved, on a sheet of paper. Then form the psychic matrix in consciousness in which you remove the problem and build in its place the positive condition you wish to invoke.

How to build an entirely new life

To build an entirely new life in the future, you can create the psychic matrix embodying the elements you wish in your new life. Here is how you build this psychic matrix for this purpose:

1. Go into the psychic silence with a complete catalogue of the new life you wish to live. Choose the type of work you would like to be in, the amount of money you wish to make, the types of friends you wish to associate with, the home that you desire, the location you would like to live in, the possessions you want, the gifts and talents you would like to develop and any other elements that you would like in your new life.

2. To help you form the psychic matrix more easily and to concentrate your psychic energies on creating the new life, I suggest that you actually cut out pictures from magazines and newspapers of the things you want in your future life. Here are some instances where this psychic matrix worked to create what was pictured by the persons concerned:

One young man of fifteen desired a strong muscular body. He concentrated on pictures of Steve Reeves, who was Mr. Universe, and projected the psychic image that he would be strong and muscular. He was guided to a course of body building which achieved his objective and a few years later he was chosen Mr. America!

A young lady wanted to become a singer of popular songs; she cut out pictures of famous singers, got their records and played them over and over, getting their vibrations in her psychic brain centers. She studied singing for a year, and finally wound up singing with a combination that made records, and is now one of our most popular recording artists!

3. Concentrate every day for at least half an hour in building your psychic matrix with the following instructions to your higher mind, embodying the elements you desire in your new life for the future:

I now break the mold of the past, with its negativity, failure, poverty and unhappiness. I create the new psychic matrix for my future life, in which I build on the principles of security, happiness, success and fulfillment in all departments of my life. I project a new job, a better income, financial security, health, happiness, social activity and romantic fulfillment.

To build a magnetic and dynamic personality in the psychic matrix, so you can become a leader of others and attract people of influence and importance, take these steps:

Go into the psychic silence and concentrate the power of your higher mind on the qualities that make one more magnetic: generosity, goodness, honesty, beauty, love, happiness and optimism. Then place these qualities in the psychic matrix of your higher consciousness, through affirming them and making them real.

I now project in the psychic matrix of the cosmos the quality of generosity and charity, knowing that as I give, so shall I receive. I now give smiles, kindness, and consideration to everyone I meet and in return receive love and friendship.

HOW A MILLION DOLLARS WORTH OF
REAL ESTATE WAS SOLD BY BUILDING THE
PSYCHIC MATRIX OF A MAGNETIC VOICE

A young man to whom I taught this system of building the phychic matrix was a weak, vacillating person, with no great talent. He spoke in a weak, timid voice and his personality reflected the indecision he felt. He went into the psychic silence for guidance. He was told to enroll in a public speaking course in evening school. Then he was guided into taking a course in real estate. He soon became a dynamic, magnetic person, speaking in a compelling and charming voice. He became one of the most successful real estate salesmen on the West Coast, selling a million dollars worth of real estate in one year among the wealthiest Beverly Hills and Bel-Air clientele.

You can form the psychic matrix for attracting more money, important people, or objects that you wish to attract into your orbit of experience. Here is how you do this:

1. Magnetize money and objects that you wish to attract. Do this by studying the lives of rich men like Rockefeller, Morgan, Vanderbilt, Getty, Baruch, Ford, and Morgenthau. Fill the psychic matrix with the formulas they used. Get books from the library which tell their secrets of success, and let them sink into the psychic matrix of your higher mind.

2. Concentrate on duplicating the qualities these successful men have possessed. As you form the psychic matrix in these qualities, your higher mind will be automatically guided into paths that can bring you riches and success.

Most of these successful men had these qualities:

Curiosity	Patience	Unselfish desire
Determination	Optimism	Love of humanity
Perseverance	Faith	Emotional intensity
Confidence	Enthusiasm	Capacity for hard work
Vision	Goodness	
Ambition	Happiness	Acquisitiveness
		Charity

194

Here is a working plan for locating lost or hidden treasures:

1. If you have lost an object of value, do not become excited and add to your confusion. Go into the psychic silence, and ask the Cosmic Mind to assist you. Affirm to your higher psychic mind the following:

I know that nothing is ever lost to Cosmic Mind. All things are tied to the Cosmic Intelligence by invisible lines of magnetic force. I am now in tune with the object I have lost, and ask my higher psychic centers to guide me to find the object, which still exists in time and space.

Then sit quietly or go about your regular activities, and you will be led, possibly in some unique manner, to the lost object.

2. Give these instructions to your psychic matrix:

I now command the cosmic forces to bring into my range of experience all the true treasures that are hidden in the storehouse of universal riches. I now stake my claim on these glorious golden treasures of health, happiness, friendship, love, and the joys that come from all the free gifts of nature; the beauty, education and entertainment of radio, television and movies; the enrichment of books, music, art and all public treasuries of art galleries, libraries, museums and all forms of transportation. I am as rich as Midas and possess the universe and all therein.

THE ATTAINMENT OF THE FULL
HAPPINESS OF LIVING

You can create the perfect image of love and marriage and attract your soul mate, fulfilling perfectly your desires for having your own family, a beautiful home and complete happiness in your emotional life. Take these steps to imprint these elements in your psychic matrix:

1. Take into the psychic silence for concentration the ideal image of the person you wish to attract as your soul mate. If it is some person you already know, hold his or her face in mind, and affirm these instructions to your higher psychic centers:

> I now project the emotion of love to this object of my affections, She embodies all the qualities I desire in my true soul mate. I now stir the lines of psychic force between us into creative activity, arousing in her the same emotion that I feel. I desire marriage with this person, building a home of my own, which will shelter our children and give us comfort and security for our future lives together.

2. Take into psychic reverie with you the ideal qualities that you wish to imprint on the psychic matrix. These qualities, which you should concentrate on, one at a time, are: Sincerity, goodness, truth, beauty of soul, radiance, happiness, selfishness, kindness, sympathy, consideration, patience, and understanding. Your soul will vibrate in harmony with such a person, if you truly possess these same qualities.

Summary of Chapter 14

1. The invisible psychic matrix which you can use to perform miracles in your life.

2. How you can project thought forms to the cos-mic matrix and bring them into reality.
3. A program for using the psychic matrix to build and shape your future life.
4. The psychic and biological timeclock that you can set for youth, health, happiness, long life.
5. How to create the psychic matrix for security and financial ability to make a fortune in the future.
6. How a man materialized ten thousand dollars through using this principle of the psychic matrix.
7. How you can solve your problems by using this psychic matrix and build an entire new life.
8. How a young man used the psychic matrix and sold a million dollars worth of real estate in one year.
9. The qualities rich men have possessed which you can build into your psychic matrix for success and riches.
10. How you can use the psychic matrix to create a perfect love life and happy marriage.

chapter 15

How to Renew
Your Mind and Body Through
Psychic Regeneration

Ponce de Leon searched for the fountain of youth, believing that its miraculous waters would give him complete physical regeneration and long life.

Today men search for chemical formulas and scientific means to achieve the same objective. They search everywhere but within for this great secret of psychic regeneration which can give new life, energy and longevity to the brain and body cells.

You possess a psychic force within your body which can give you healing, if you should become sick.

You can regenerate your body every two years—for all the thirty billion or more cells are reborn in that time. Your body is literally never more than two years old at any time in your life!

HOW YOU CAN TAP COSMIC ENERGY
AND MAGNETISM

There is an invisible stream of cosmic energy particles and magnetism which bombards the earth from outer space, causing all living things to grow and evolve. This radiant life force is cosmic magnetism, and it can be channeled by human beings in such quantities that it regenerates the mind and body and gives one youthful vitality, long life and health when it is correctly used. When it is short-circuited by negative psychic forces it creates imbalance in the body's glandular system and the organism is deprived of harmonious cosmic life energy. It is then that the human body becomes sick, out of tune with the cosmic rhythm of life, health and youth, and dies prematurely.

We shall now study these psychic and cosmic forces which control the rhythm of life, and see how we can implement the positive elements and mitigate the negative ones which cause the body to deteriorate and grow old prematurely.

HOW PSYCHIC SHORT-CIRCUITING STUNTED CHILDREN'S NORMAL GROWTH

A study of thirteen children conducted by Johns Hopkins University School of Medicine reported that when the normal life rhythm is interrupted through negative psychic emotions, the children grew abnormally slowly. These children were in homes where the parents quarreled constantly. The children were so upset psychically and emotionally by these disturbances that their glands were adversely affected and they literally stopped their normal growth.

When these children were taken out of their disturbed environments and placed in a convalescent home, their rate of growth was accelerated remarkably.

After the children were returned to their homes once more, their rate of growth was once more retarded. Chemical studies showed that these children, due to the emotional and psychic strain they were under, secreted very small amounts of hormones which control the rate of growth from the pituitary gland.

HOW PSYCHIC CENTERS CONTROL YOUR BODY'S FUNCTIONS

The higher psychic centers of your brain are capable of controlling your growth, metabolism, body functions, digestion, assimilation, circulation of the blood, the healing rate of the body, and many other vital functions, without your conscious effort. Your breathing goes on night and day, so does your beating heart, and you make no conscious effort whatsoever about digesting the food you eat at mealtimes.

This higher psychic intelligence within you can be impeded or accelerated, depending on what conscious use you make of your emotions, and how you draw upon the cosmic magnetism in the invisible, which causes all life to grow. It is now known scientifically that magnetism and electricity in the body cells are the two invisible cosmic elements which give man life.

HOW SHORT-CIRCUITING OCCURS IN THE BRAIN AND BODY

What forces contribute to the short-circuiting of this cosmic life force known as magnetism?

These are known now to scientists, and it is believed by most modern biologists and bio-chemists, that if these negative forces were removed from the mind and body, man could easily live to be two hundred years of age or more.

These negative short-circuiting emotions that inhabit the consciousness destroy the magnetism and electricity in the brain and body cells. They cause the psychic and intuitive power that is inherent in all living cells to be subverted and the cells lose their ability to regenerate and stay young. Acids accumulate in the blood and tissues and the body becomes old before its time, loses its capacity to fight germs, and sickness ensues, bringing a shorter life span, and premature death.

THE NEGATIVE EMOTIONS THAT DESTROY COSMIC MAGNETISM

The following negative emotions destroy cosmic magnetism and set the stage for sickness, premature old age, accident and death. If you can rid your mind of these negative forces, the normal psychic and intuitive forces within your brain and body cells will regenerate your body, and keep you young and healthy:

1) Fear
2) Hate
3) Worry
4) Resentment
5) Jealousy
6) Revenge
7) Selfishness
8) Greed
9) Envy
10) Anger
11) Pessimism
12) Frustration
13) Anxiety
14) Insecurity

These fourteen negative emotions kill cosmic magnetism and short-circuit the psychic power that tells the cells how to grow, evolve and regenerate themselves to keep the body healthy, young and vital until its full life span of a hundred years or more has been fulfilled.

HOW NEGATIVE EMOTIONS CREATE DEATH-DEALING CHEMICALS

A woman received a psychic shock that produced diabetes when a tree frog dropped into the front of her dress, causing her to become frightened.

Another case of how negative emotions work to destroy the body's chemical balance was that of a woman whose son had been pronounced dead by the War Department, who suddenly showed up at her door alive. This shock also produced a condition of diabetes.

CHEMICAL POISONING PRODUCED MONSTERS

Scientific proof of the validity of this theory came from an experiment conducted by scientists with chicken eggs. With a hypodermic needle they injected small quantities of poisons into the eggs; nicotine, alcohol and acid were used. These fertilized eggs were then allowed to germinate and hatch. After twenty-one days of incubation all the eggs hatched, but what monsters they produced! Little chicks were born without feathers; some with their hearts outside the body; others with two heads, or without eyes or legs. In every instance nature's cosmic pattern of perfection was distorted and destroyed, and monsters were created.

THE POSITIVE EMOTIONS WHICH PRODUCE LIFE-GIVING COSMIC MAGNETISM FOR HEALTH AND LONG LIFE

Just as we know which negative emotions produce the short-circuiting effects of sickness, old age and premature death, so too we know which positive emotions create the life-giving force of cosmic magnetism which can give one health, vitality, youth and a life span of a hundred or more years.

Let us now learn what these life-giving positive emotions are and use them in our daily activities. They will trigger the automatic psychic guidance from your higher mind, which will cause your body cells to generate magnetism and electricity and remain youthful and healthy until an advanced old age.

1) Love
2) Peace
3) Happiness
4) Optimism
5) Hope
6) Charity
7) Confidence
8) Unselfishness
9) Good
10) Expectation
11) Courage
12) Compassion
13) Faith
14) Security

HOW TO USE POSITIVE EMOTIONS TO BUILD COSMIC MAGNETISM AND HEALTH

Following is a program for daily application to build your health:

1. Make it a point to carefully go over the negative list of emotions and pick out those which you indulge daily. If it is *fear*, supplant it with the emotion of *confidence*. This positive emotion will trigger the psychic force within

your brain which causes you to act with courage and confidence in the face of depressing and discouraging obstacles.

2. Memorize the twenty-third and the ninety-first Psalms and repeat them whenever you feel a sense of fear or insecurity.

3. Try to charge the psychic batteries of your mind by daily passing positive emotions through the filaments of your psychic centers. Adopt a daily regime in which you feature one of the positive emotions on the above list. Pin a chart up on your wall with a week's schedule on it featuring a different positive, magnetic emotion for each day, and indulge that emotion as often as you can on that particular day. This will tend to crystalize that emotional charge of magnetism in your psychic centers and radiate to your brain and body cells its magnetic charge of life force and psychic energy. Here is how your daily chart might look;

Monday: LOVE. Today I shall live in the consciousness of love. I radiate love to everyone I meet, and forgive all those who have harmed me in any way.

Tuesday: PEACE. I enthrone the magnetic vibrations of peace in my psychic centers all day today. No one shall have the power to disturb the center of my peaceful equilibrium with any negative action this day.

Wednesday: HAPPINESS. Today I live in the conscious awareness of the emotion of happiness. I am happy and I strive to radiate happiness in my relations with others in my home, in my place of business and in contact with strangers.

Thursday: OPTIMISM. I radiate this magnetic emotion all day. I see the bright side of everything and confidently expect good from every situation which engages my attention.

Friday: HOPE. I register the emotion of hope in my higher psychic centers today. I am hopeful of the future. I radiate hope in my thinking and my speech.

Saturday: CHARITY. Today I express charitable impulses in my actions towards others. I am kind, tolerant and understanding, helping those who need help, giving of my smiles, consideration and service to everyone I meet.

Sunday: CONFIDENCE. I express the magnetic emotion of confidence all day today. I am confident in myself, and believe that I shall ultimately find my right destiny through psychic guidance.

4. Use deep breathing and rhythmic, magnetic walking to draw into your body the magnetism which is in the cosmos. You can breathe in slowly to the count of ten, hold the breath for four counts, as you magnetically tense your entire body, then release the breath to the count of four. Do this whenever you feel the need of regenerating your body and ridding it of the cumulative toxic wastes and poisons. When you arise in the morning you should practice this psychic regenerative breathing, and all during the day, instead of smoking or taking cocktails to renew your energy, stop and breathe ten or fifteen times, drawing deeply into your lungs with diaphragmatic breathing, the golden elixir of life. This oxygen you breathe is filled with magnetism, electricity and radioactive substances which give your body energy and keep it alive and healthy.

5. Learn to slow down the excess metabolism of your body by controlled, slow breathing when you are in a relaxed state. The tortoise breathes only two or three times a minute and lives to be from one hundred to two hundred years of age; a dove breathes twenty-five or thirty times a minute and its life span is short. Slow breathing, when in periods of psychic reverie, will help build psychic and cosmic magnetism in your body cells, and slow down your metabolism to the cosmic rhythm of long life, youth, health and vitality.

6. Learn how to relax and let the cosmic magnetism in your brain and body cells accumulate. This will help remove the toxic wastes from your body. Western civilization is killing itself off by being overly ambitious and money mad.

7. Have confidence in the higher psychic guidance that can come through to you, which can cause you to protect yourself from dangers that might threaten your health or your life. You should sit every day in the psychic silence to

receive guidance for that day. You will be told intuitively through psychic means how to live your life, what foods to eat and how to avert danger that might threaten your life.

8. Follow your own higher psychic guidance as to what you should eat, how you should exercise, what habits you should build to maintain your body at high levels of energy, to offset old age and to preserve the life force for at least one hundred years of useful, active living.

The higher psychic mind within you knows what you should eat, how you should live, *if nothing interferes with its communication of intuitive intelligence.*

Why people can live to be over one hundred

A scientific study has been made of one hundred and sixty-five people who had lived to be a hundred years of age or more, and it was discovered that most of these people had lived all their lives under the guidance of intuition. They had not followed any one set of rules in diet or exercise, but did the things that they felt (psychical guidance) were right for them. Here were the general rules under which they lived; some of these might be adopted by you to help guide your actions to longer life and better health.

a) These people ate what they felt like eating, with no special preferences or harsh diet disciplines.

b) They ate when they felt the urge for nutrition, not satisfaction, and did not over-eat.

c) They worked hard, as a rule, all their lives, and never worried too much about exercise as such.

d) They were usually religious people who had faith in God or in some strong belief.

e) They were generally calm and unemotional about life, seldom gave in to temper and violent fits of emotion.

f) They were usually happily married, and family affairs engaged much of their time.

g) They were usually in moderate circumstances, but felt secure and happy in their limited financial conditions.

h) They had limited social activities, and did not indulge much in cocktail parties and other group activities.

i) Most of them did not drink alcohol or smoke cigarettes, but the few who did, smoked and drank in moderation.

j) They seldom took medicines or visited doctors, and had fewer ailments than people who were constantly worried about health.

k) They were usually optimistic and expectant of good.

l) They had a spiritual philosophy which caused them to believe in a hereafter and a God. There were no athiests among them.

m) They were people who lived quiet lives, were seldom restless or nervous and did not have a desire to travel or do unusual things. Most of them were homebodies.

FOLLOW YOUR OWN PSYCHIC GUIDANCE IN MATTERS OF HEALTH AND LONG LIFE

If you follow psychic guidance in matters of health and life, you will be guided to do the right things at the right time to give you cosmic magnetism, health and vitality. If you take care not to short-circuit your psychic life energy with negative emotions and taking poisons into your system, you can preserve the psychic life urge for a hundred years of healthy, vibrant, useful life. Most of our modern illnesses are due to strain, worry, fear, and wrong dietary and breathing habits. Your higher psychic mind can guide you to do the right things if you practice daily sessions to receive this psychic and intuitive guidance.

Summary of Chapter 15

1. How you may tap the invisible stream of cosmic energy and magnetism which bombards the earth from outer space.
2. Children's growth stunted through confusion and negative emotions.
3. The forces that cause short-circuiting in the brain and body and produce sickness and short life.

4. The fourteen negative emotions that destroy cosmic magnetism and shorten life.

5. How negative emotions create death-dealing chemicals that unbalance the glands and produce sickness.

6. Science produced monsters through injecting chemical poisons in chicken eggs.

7. The positive emotions which produce life-giving cosmic magnetism for health and long life.

8. The fourteen positive emotions that generate magnetism and electricity in your body cells and give you health and long life.

9. How to use positive emotions to build cosmic magnetism.

10. The seven-day regime for building psychic power and magnetism to add years to your life.

11. One hundred and sixty-five case histories of people who lived a hundred or more years and how they kept healthy.

12. How to follow your own psychic promptings in matters of health, diet and long life.

chapter 16

How to Attract
and Influence
People Important to You

You have the power to project your thought forms to
people you want to meet and attract them into the orbit of
your environment and experience.

You can hold conversations with important people psychically, and tune in on their wavelengths and receive in-
information from their minds.

You have the power to psychically contact any important person in the world and magnetize him or her, and
even meet the person—if you choose.

I have used this power all my life and psychically attuned my mind to meeting the most important people in
the world—they came and *sought me out* as though they
had been given some kind of secret cosmic command to
do so!

YOUR MIND AS A SENDING AND
RECEIVING STATION

Your mind is a receiving station as well as a psychic
sending station. You can reach out in time and space and
touch the minds of others through telepathic communication, when you might not be able to actually contact the
person physically. This type of psychic communication
can be with important people in key positions that you
wish to contact or influence.

The Cosmic Mind is a vast network of electrical and
magnetic currents that flows throughout the body cells of
the cosmos, motivating them, shaping them and creating
constant new forms and patterns through psychic communication.

HOW COSMIC TELEPATHY WORKS IN
ALL NATURE

There are communities of insects, such as bees, ants, and termites, which seem to communicate with each other through some form of telepathy. For instance, a group of bees will set about, as if by some pre-arranged psychic signal, to make the royal jelly that will cause some of the larva which feed on it to turn into queens who will be the leaders of new swarms of bees, forming their own future communities.

Other bees have a strange psychic compulsion to gorge themselves with honey, so they can create the essential wax which they require to build their hives and store honey. If a snail or mouse invades the hive the bees instantly mobilize their forces to overpower the enemy, sting it to death, and then—most miraculous instinct of all—coat the body with wax, a perfect embalming to keep the invader from decaying and poisoning the hive. How can these tiny creatures receive these psychic instructions except through some kind of cosmic network of telepathic intelligence and communication which pervades the entire universe?

A TELEPATHIC SYSTEM EXISTS WITHIN
YOUR BODY CELLS

Now let us carry our cosmic hypothesis a step further, and realize that all these creatures in nature, including the highest form of creation—man, use some kind of telepathic system of signalling to the complicated structure of body cells which make up their organisms. Indeed, this psychic signalling seems to be a part of all biological systems, which causes cells to signal to each other when they need certain chemicals. Evidence exists that the neurones of the body, especially the cells of the endocrine organs, are capable of signalling to the other organs when they require certain chemicals or wish to perform various changes in their embryonic growth.

We see this psychic and telepathic communication within the body cells, as organized intelligent members of a community, when they cause the blood to circulate throughout the body, when they transform solid foods into brain and body tissue; and when the white blood corpuscles organize in a solid body to attack invading bacteria which might cause sickness or death.

A PSYCHO-COSMIC BODY POSSESSES THE SAME POWER OF PSYCHIC AND COSMIC TELEPATHY

Human beings might be called highly organized *cells of a vast cosmic body* which possesses the same power of psychic and cosmic telepathy among its members as the body does among its cells.

Therefore, *we are all inter-related* by this cosmic network of sensitized intelligence and we may communicate with others as well as with the Cosmic Mind which governs all creation.

There is a kind of cosmic or psychic blueprint that exists between all members of a species. In human beings this form of psychic communication is determined by common behavior patterns, universal desires and emotions, and instinctive urges, such as the hunger urge, the love urge, the social urge, and the spiritual urge. This cosmic plan, which flows telepathically throughout the entire human race, manifests itself in all human beings with the same urges and desires.

Time and space are no obstacles to this telepathic cosmic communication, for thoughts are electrical and go forth faster than the speed of light to reach their objective.

HOW I MET THE DUKE AND DUCHESS OF WINDSOR THROUGH PSYCHIC PROJECTION

I had long wanted to meet the Duke and Duchess of Windsor so I could photograph them and do a magazine article about them. In 1956, I went to Vienna, and after holding this psychic projection in mind for about two years, I was invited to a party at the Balkan Grill, a famous restaurant in Vienna; the Duke and Duchess of Windsor were the honored guests!

The Duke and Duchess gave me permission to take pictures, and I sat and chatted informally with them for three hours. They were having their memoirs published by a big publisher, and the Duke kindly consented to send me to their publisher to do one of my early books. This entire meeting could *not have been arranged by human agencies.* It had to come about through psychic influence and energy. If you form the picture and project the image to the Cosmic Mind, of what you wish to do and whom you wish to meet—in some mysterious way the psychic thought will be projected into the dimensions of reality and be fulfilled.

REGIME FOR USING PSYCHIC AND COSMIC TELEPATHY TO INFLUENCE AND ATTRACT IMPORTANT PEOPLE

You will be delighted with the results of applying the following program:

1. Psychic and cosmic telepathy deal with emotions and thought forms. When you go into the psychic silence to practice this form of mental projection to a person you wish to reach, be certain that you hold the face of that person in the forefront of your consciousness. If you have a picture of the person it will be even better to help you imprint the form in your consciousness.

2. Mentally see a golden line between your eyes and the person's eyes, and as you pull this line up from the center, see the face coming closer and closer to you. Then send out the psychic message you wish to imprint on the other person's psychic centers. Speak the name to yourself, say it over several times; then follow it with your message.

For example, it may be the head of a company where you wish employment. You will say the person's name: "Mr. R., I am sending you this message. You will receive the psychic thought forms that I am projecting. I wish to work for your company. I will make application for the

211

job of assistant manager. I have valuable assets which will benefit your company. I know that I can perform my duties capably and I will do credit to your organization. I desire a salary of $15,000 a year, with suitable promotions and advancement over the years. I am steady, of sober habits, and good character. I shall be proud to be associated with your company. You will favorably consider me for this job."

3. After you have projected your psychic thought forms try to feel the emotion of fulfillment. Know within yourself that you will have the job; feel the satisfaction that comes from accomplishment. See yourself in the office, with your own desk, doing your work, being accepted by the other employees.

4. Prepare the psychic groundwork for meeting with this person who is important to your future welfare. Hold a psychic conversation with him; ask questions, wait for answers; hold his face in the forefront of your mind as you talk things over with him. You may not feel that you can communicate with a person in this way, but remember— *your soul substance and his soul substance are of the same vibratory pattern.* In the vast network of Cosmic Intelligence ALL THOUGHT FORMS ARE INTERRELATED, and the Cosmic Mind knows the thoughts of the person you are trying to reach because of the universality of all human emotions and communications.

5. Just as you might write a letter to an important person stating your qualifications, qualities and desirable traits, so too you can have astral and psychic communication with an important person you wish to attract or influence. Write a letter to that person, stating all your thoughts as clearly as if you were speaking to him in person. Tell him why you wish to meet him, what your plans are, how you will benefit him, and how you are motivated by unselfish desire and sincerity.

6. When you are trying to reach some important person, (by important I mean one who is important to you, not necessarily someone in high office or a position of power) project your psychic thoughts in words, for remember thoughts are clothed in words before they can be communicated psychically. If you hold just a vague

thought that you would like to meet some person or have someone do something for you, it will not easily lodge in that person's psychic centers to produce the action you desire. We are creatures of word communication, and you can reach a person psychically on the verbal level by projecting the message in the actual words you wish to send.

7. Salesmen in any field may use this psychic and telepathic communication with their customers. Your thoughts should be projected directly to the person, linking your mind with his, and even while he is objecting or resisting your sale you can project the psychic command: "You will see the merits of this product. You will buy it, for it will be of benefit and value to you. You will no longer resist my sales talk, but agree fully that you want and need this product."

How a jewelry salesman sold with psychic projection

A jewelry salesman who dealt mostly with women used this psychic projection with every customer. When a woman was about to buy a very expensive piece of jewelry, usually accompanied by her husband or some other man, there would be resistance to the sale. This man, who was versed in psychic salesmanship, would look at the woman, just between the eyes, and project a golden line of infinity, over which he would project this telepathic message:

"You will buy this piece of jewelry. Think how beautiful it will look on you. It was created to make your type of woman more beautiful."

8. This psychic communication is especially valuable when you wish to reach some large manufacturer or company to buy an invention or carry out some creative idea that you may have. You can easily find out the name of the head of the company to whom you wish to sell your product or invention through industrial information services. Psychically rehearse all your dialogue with the head of this company before you keep your appointment with him. Tell him of the merits of your idea or invention; impress upon him the money he will make through it, the need for this product, the glory and pleasure he will receive from

developing it. Then, when you are in the man's presence, keep up your psychic dialogue, ignoring any negative comments he makes, but insisting psychically that he take your idea or invention and manufacture it.

How an electrical gadget was sold

A man I know had an invention for improving an electrical appliance that had already been manufactured. He kept projecting the psychic message that someone in the electrical manufacturing line should seek him out. Without making any special effort, other than going into psychic reverie and silence daily for a half hour, he was invited one night to a friend's home for dinner. There he was introduced to a man who ran one of the biggest outlets for electrical appliances of the type this man wanted to improve with his invention. He made his thoughts known to this electrical supply man who told him he knew a big manufacturer who would consider the man's invention. A meeting was arranged, and the inventor found himself saying the words, and listening to the very arguments that he had projected in his psychic reverie! The outcome was that this man got a contract to manufacture his electrical gadget that eventually brought him two hundred and fifty thousand dollars and a royalty payment on each item sold for the rest of his life.

HOW I PROJECTED A MEETING WITH WILLIAM RANDOLPH HEARST

I remember once, when I was just starting my career in Hollywood, I wanted to meet the noted multi-millionaire publisher, William Randolph Hearst, but so did everyone else in Hollywood. Mr. Hearst just was not available, for his time was too valuable and he was protected from the general public.

I worked for three months on projecting thought forms and telepathic messages to Mr. Hearst, telling him why I wanted to meet him and urging him to help me when we did meet.

One day Mary Pickford invited me to a party at Pickfair for some famous people; the guests of honor were Lord and Lady Mountbatten of England. I went to this party and was introduced to William Randolph Hearst. He turned out to be charming and most interesting. Our conversation lasted for over half an hour, and it was along the lines that *I had projected in my psychic reverie!*

From that meeting came a completely new career, for Mr. Hearst gave me the front page of the *American Weekly Magazine* for *four weeks in a row!* This had never been given to any individual in the history of that publication. He publicized my book *You and the Stars* which sold many thousands of copies. Then, as I had scheduled in my psychic projection, every year after that the Hearst papers carried stories giving my psychic and astrological predictions for the movie greats.

Summary of Chapter 16

1. How you can use your higher psychic centers for receiving and sending thoughts to important people.
2. How to use the vast network of psychic communication which is in all creation for your greater good.
3. Scientists prove that psychic power connects all people.
4. The cosmic blueprint which is in nature and which you may prefabricate and use for your future.
5. How to use psychic and cosmic telepathy to influence and attract important people.
6. How you can project the golden line of infinity to other's minds and influence them.
7. How you can give psychic commands that will be obeyed.
8. How you can hold psychic communication with others through projecting thought forms and ideas.

chapter 17

How to Contact
Geniuses of the Past
Through Psychic Attunement

What wouldn't you give to be able to talk to great geniuses of the past and receive information and guidance from their illumined minds?

Think of being able to tune in on the mind of Galileo and discover his innermost secret thoughts.

How wonderful if you could tune in on the minds of Leonardo da Vinci or Michelangelo and learn their great secrets in creative art.

Think of how wonderful it would be to tap the mind of Vanderbilt or J. P. Morgan and learn their secrets for building a fortune.

Edison, Lincoln, Columbus, Einstein, Carnegie and George Washington Carver—*all these geniuses still exist in some dimension of time and space and you can attune your psychic antenna to their thoughts and be guided by them in your life!*

You possess a psychic antenna which can be attuned to any wavelength of psychic reception and which can receive information and guidance from geniuses of the past.

As a radio or television set may be tuned to receive various stations, so too, this higher psychic center of your mind can be attuned to great thoughts and inspirations, creative ideas and sources of wisdom and power which can make you a creative genius.

HOW PSYCHIC POWER GIVES MAN
WINGS OF THE SOUL

"Man shall grow wings," Leonardo da Vinci wrote under his sketch of the first airplane over four hundred years ago.

217

Man tapped the source of power from the infinite and literally grew wings—jet wings, space wings—which enable him to soar through the atmosphere at two thousand miles per hour.

We span the globe with our projected radio and television beams in a few seconds' time, and are able to transmit sounds and forms in color, that would astound the minds of past generations. We dial a phone number and hear a human voice across continents and oceans within seconds.

We peer through our electronic telescopes at Palomar and see the heavenly bodies brought amazingly close to earth. What a magnificent creation that issued from the mind of Galileo, whose mind first conceived and perfected the principle of the telescope.

We look through our electronic microscopes, and see whole new worlds of form and color magnified to astounding proportions, and gain new insight into the very secrets of life itself. Scientists at long last have used the psychic inspiration of men like Pasteur and Newton and Edison to give us new understanding of the mysterious world in which we live.

We peer into the secret heart of nature's products, and learn how to form new combinations of atoms and molecules and change the very nature of matter, creating new chemicals and wonderful new products which mankind may use. We are still tapping the same psychic strata of infinite intelligence which Burbank and other forerunners in his field were able to channel.

YOUR SOUL'S REMEMBRANCE OF THE PAST

Your soul can be attuned to the psychic wavelength of these great men who have gone on to other realms, and have remembrances of things past. No thought or inspiration ever dies. Just as the rosebud lives on in the seed that will bloom in the spring, even though snow covers the earth in wintertime, so too, the soul's remembrance of its immortality and greatness survives the chilling winds and bleak despair of death's winter. It knows its own destiny in the springtime of hope and faith and life which exists in another dimension of time and space.

You can choose your own *psychic mentor* from the realm of the invisible, and attune yourself to the same wavelengths that enabled him to create. You can be guided by his psychic thought forces, just as a teacher here on earth can direct you and fill your mind with knowledge, inspiration and desire to achieve.

INVISIBLE PHANTOM THOUGHT FORMS ARE ALL AROUND YOU

The room in which you now sit is filled with invisible music, the sound of voices and invisible phantom forms. You might argue that the room is totally empty and that you are its only occupant. You cannot hear or see the whirlwind of confusion, nor hear the incessant chatter of human voices, because it is effectively screened out of your consciousness by barriers interposed by matter. However, with a flip of a switch, and by turning a little knob, you can enter another dimension of sound and space where you become attuned to the invisible forms and hear the phantom voices, music and sounds that bombard time and space continuously. You have simply tuned in your radio or television to the dimension where these forces exist. You have made them a reality by entering their world of soundless spirit.

This is the process which geniuses of the past have also used when they have tapped invisible dimensions of time and space, and channelized music, art, poetry, literature, inventions and new products, which they have wrested from the womb of time. They tuned in to the invisible realm of cosmic spirit and found the specific wavelength which gave them the inspiration to produce and create the masterpieces which make us think them geniuses.

1.   First know the genius whose thought forms you wish to receive with your higher psychic centers. You can only know him through a study of his life and works; his habits, his friends, his emotional values, his beliefs and prejudices. Pick the particular genius you wish to receive psychic thought forms from; study his life and works through the public library. Read every book you can find about him, and then go into the psychic silence and attune your soul's wavelength to his by concentrating on him and his creative thoughts. By the law of magnetic and psychic attraction, you will find yourself attracting thoughts and ideas that are amazingly like the genius you have selected.

2.   Make out a list, similar to the one below, of some of the world's greatest geniuses and their achievements, so that you will have guidance in your choice of the source from which you will receive information and inspiration. You may choose as many of these geniuses for psychic contact as you wish, and then, after studying their lives and works, you can proceed to make contact with the vibratory thought patterns which still exist in the cosmos and which issued from their inspired minds.

Pythagoras, the great mathematician, who discovered the vibratory theory back of matter and knew of its atomic and molecular structure

Galileo, who discovered that the earth revolved around the sun, not the sun around the earth, and who created the first telescope

Newton, who first proved the law of gravity, which Galileo had explored in his experiments (This great discovery by Newton, that some strange, magnetic force in matter existed, paved the way for man to create his heavier-than-air machines which could rise above the gravity pull of earth and soar into the heavens.)

Columbus, who dared explore unknown worlds and proved the world was round, not flat, as was then thought

Benjamin Franklin, who proved the existence of electricity, and who was a brilliant writer, statesman and inventor

Edison, who was one of the greatest inventors of all time

Burbank, who probed nature's secrets and gave us many new fruits, vegetables and flowers through his knowledge of grafting and cross-pollination

The *Wright Brothers,* who developed the airplane and first flew it successfully

Einstein, who paved the way to our atomic age with his theory of relativity, in which he proved the spiritual nature of matter and its actual non-existence

Fleming and Salk, who brought Pasteur's theories and discoveries in the field of protective vaccines to new and more glorious reality with their discoveries of penicillin and polio vaccine

Mme. Curie and her husband, who isolated radium

Albert Schweitzer, whose genius advanced the cause of science and medicine in healing the primitive tribes of Africa

Ghandi of India, whose genius liberated his nation

Socrates, Plato and Aristotle, who advanced the frontiers of man's philosophical knowledge with their great revelations

Darwin, who brought order out of chaos with his theories of evolution and differentiation of the species, which changed modern scientific concepts about the creation of the world

Marconi, Alexander Graham Bell, and David Sarnoff, who contributed to the modern telegraph, telephone, radio and television through their genius and experimentation.

Disraeli and Churchill, whose leadership and statesmanship gave the world new concepts in political philosophy

221

Lincoln and Washington, who brought freedom and unity to our nation and liberated millions of people from slavery and political domination

Rembrandt, Michelangelo, Leonard da Vinci, Raphael, and Titian, the artistic geniuses, who revealed such magnificent concepts in art that they changed the standards of the world for all time to come

Shakespeare, Milton, Keats, Shelley, Byron, Dickens, Balzac and Flaubert, who brought their great genius to poetry, literature and drama, and released inspiration for man's noblest utterances in the realm of human emotion

Beethoven, Chopin, Handel, Mozart and Bach, who crystallized the cosmic music of the spheres into celestial vibrations which will continue to bless the minds and hearts of men for an eternity

Then, in making out your list of geniuses whose inspiration you wish to tap with your higher psychic mind, do not forget to include the great financial geniuses and business experts who have given the world vast treasures which have enriched all our lives: *Vanderbilt, Morgan, Rockefeller, Ford, Carnegie and Sears.*

3.   When you have made out a list of the great geniuses whose psychic guidance you desire in your own life, put these geniuses into categories, and choose the one which fits your particular form of creative talent. A rough category might look this this:

Businessmen	Artists
Statesmen and leaders	Composers and musicians
Inventors	Authors, poets and dramatists
Scientists	Singers, actors, dancers, designers

4.   Now choose the category and the persons who fit this category, and deliberately go about studying their lives; obtain biographies and autobiographies from the library. Learn how these geniuses lived and thought. Fill your mind with their words and philosophies. Practice their daily habit patterns of work and play. In other words,

222

put yourself on the same wavelength psychically that these geniuses lived on while they were here on earth.

5. After you have filled your consciousness with the psychic wavelengths of the particular genius you wish to receive guidance and information from, sit in the psychic silence for at least an hour. Hold in your mind the thought forms that you know are typical of this person. Then use the following form to address this person's cosmic and psychic thought forces, which still exist in time and space. Let us say that you have selected someone like Lincoln for psychic guidance and inspiration. You would say to your higher psychic centers, "I now wish to contact the cosmic wavelength of Abraham Lincoln, for inspiration and guidance in my own life. I am in tune now with the qualities of vision, justice, unity and forgiveness. I wish to contact the psychic thought forms of Lincoln for solving my own personal problems."

6. Then state the particular problem on which you wish guidance or information. When you have projected your questions to the psychic mind of Lincoln, sit quietly and wait for answers and solutions. Your psychic centers will begin to vibrate in harmony with the thoughts and inspirations of Lincoln. You may receive a direct message at the time, which will come to you in the form of thoughts and ideas, or may come as an inner voice, which will answer your questions or solve your problems.

7. If you wish to hold a special psychic conference with several minds, you can call up the psychic phantom forms of several advisors and these geniuses will all contribute their thoughts and inspirations. For instance, you might want to tune in on the wavelengths of Disraeli, Benjamin Franklin, and Einstein—a truly formidable conference can occur when you once assemble the cosmic thought forms of these three great geniuses. You have already studied their lives and works; you are in tune with their wavelengths psychically. You can hold your mind still while one and all of these three geniuses radiate their psychic thought forms to your higher mind centers.

8. If you choose the category of inspiration that is represented by business and financial leaders, you would enlist the aid of possibly Carnegie, Rockefeller and Mor-

gan, three of our great modern geniuses in the financial field. You would project your psychic wavelengths to the Cosmic Mind, asking for specific guidance and information from these three geniuses. As you have already studied the lives of these three financial wizards, you are already in psychic attunement with their cosmic forces. You can ask of Carnegie such questions as: "How can I build my future fortune? What investments should I make? Should I go into this business I plan? Then you can sit quietly and await the answers to your questions. If no particular answers come in that moment, go about your daily activities, and perhaps the answer will come later, through a book you will read on investments, your mind will suddenly receive a psychic nudge. This is a form of delayed psychic reaction which shows that Cosmic Mind never forgets to give you specific guidance, but it may choose a time and place which suits its particular needs. You must be alert to these psychic promptings at unusual or unexpected times.

Edison often was awakened by this type of psychic nudge and given the answer to some troublesome inventive problem.

9. You might ask of Rockefeller the following questions about your financial or business matters: "What field of endeavor am I best suited to? How can I build financial security for my family and myself? Is it wise to invest in real estate or stocks and bonds at the present time?"

Having put yourself in tune with the Rockefeller vibrations through a study of his life and habits, you will be on his psychic wavelength and may receive direct or delayed action guidance on the questions you ask him.

10. Be sure that you use psychic motivators which fit the particular genius you have chosen to be your psychic mentor. There are several of these psychic motivators which all geniuses have used. The most powerful ones are the following:

A desire to better yourself and your family.
A desire to educate your children in the future.

A desire to get rich so you can help alleviate the world's suffering.

A desire to elevate the standards of the world.

A desire to bring peace and brotherhood to the world.

A love of humanity and a love of God, with the desire to serve humanity and God.

Rockefeller and Carnegie had a desire to get rich to better themselves and their families, it is true, but they had a secondary psychic motivator which was to help alleviate the world's suffering, to elevate the standards of the world. Carnegie spent over five hundred million dollars in his lifetime to help evolve the standards of the world through art, music, and culture. He gave the famous Carnegie Hall to New York City; he endowed twelve hundred public libraries to give wisdom and knowledge to the world.

11. If you wish to receive the psychic wavelengths of great inspirational music, go into the silence, and ask for inspiration from Beethoven or Chopin. Put recordings on your record player of these geniuses' works. Fill your consciousness with the musical beauty and inspiration that they poured forth and then ask one or both to give you guidance for playing the piano, composing songs, or in other ways duplicating their musical genius.

There are psychic overtones in the cosmos of all great creative ideas; music has such an overtone, and it will stir into creative inspiration and action your own higher psychic wavelengths and centers when you expose yourself to the beauty and rhythm of their great music.

12. If you wish to consult with a genius like Shakespeare for purposes of writing great drama or literature, fill your psychic centers with the language he used in his works. Then sit in the silence and ask for psychic guidance from his thought forces. The same power that Shakespeare used to inspire him is in the Cosmic Memory bank, and can reach out and touch the fountainhead of your own creative energy and inspiration.

You might study the lives of such dramatists as Shaw or Ibsen if you wish to be guided by the psychic overtones of their great creative genius.

HOW ONE WRITER TUNED IN ON THOMAS WOLFE

I know one such writer who used this technique for enriching his writing, and he asked for guidance from Thomas Wolfe, who died in the late thirties. To receive psychic guidance from this acknowledged literary genius of our modern age, he read the books that Wolfe had written and he studied the author's published letters, and a book written about the famous author by his sister. Then he sat in regular psychic sessions before his typewriter and asked for psychic guidance from Thomas Wolfe. Brilliant writing came through him, and it was *not an imitation of Thomas Wolfe,* but of an original style colored by the personality of the writer who was under psychic guidance. This young man sold his first novel, and it was made into a movie for which he received one hundred thousand dollars. He can write as many books as he wishes to, using the psychic overtones of any of the great geniuses in the literary world, past or present.

13. When you concentrate on the psychic wavelength of any genius, you automatically magnetize and attract the thought forms that were crystallized in the Cosmic Memory bank by that person. Vibratory thought patterns are impressed upon the cosmic protoplasm of vibration and atomic energy, and are capable of being transmitted through time and space just as electricity, magnetism and cosmic radiation are transmitted. A snowflake carries out this theory perfectly; it is invisible moisture until some vibratory force crystallizes the drops of water into a lace-like, visible structure, which has form, size, shape and dimension, that is, third-dimensional. So too, the radiatory thought waves of geniuses exist in a vibratory dimension until they are imprinted with creative patterns by the Cosmic Intelligence, as directed by some motivating force, like human will or desire. You may tap these invisible

226

thought forms from the minds of geniuses and shape them into new and amazing creative patterns by imprinting upon them your own individuality and originality.

HOW AN ATTORNEY WINS COURT CASES THROUGH THIS PRINCIPLE

I know one young attorney who uses this secret of psychic imprinting by drawing upon the minds of great lawyers of the past for his inspiration and guidance when he is pleading a case in the courtroom. He has, to date, won 95 percent of all his criminal cases. He takes some great genius from the past, whose life he has studied thoroughly, and asks him for psychic guidance before going into the courtroom. It might be a Disraeli, a Gladstone or a Clarence Darrow—it does not matter which, but he chooses one particular psychic mentor for that particular case. He goes into psychic reverie for a half hour or so, and garners all the information he can from the thought forms of the particular person he is asking for help. Then, when he is in the courtroom, he transfigures his mind and body into the person he has chosen for his mentor; thinking, feeling, acting, and speaking as his higher psychic centers guide him—which, of course, is in the psychic image of the genius he has selected.

AN ARTIST DRAWS ON THE INSPIRATION OF TURNER

Then there is an artist friend of mine, who is famous for his seascapes and his bright, glowing sunrise and sunset scenes. He visits the Metropolitan Museum of Art in New York City, at least once a month, studying all the great geniuses of the past and their artistic masterpieces. He is especially fond of the seascapes of Turner, and he has made it a point to study the life and works of this great genius thoroughly. When he sits before his canvas to paint, he invokes the psychic mentor of Turner's psychic thought forces, and feels that the great artist actually guides him in his work.

When you psychically attune yourself to the highest, most inspiring, noblest and most magnificent psychic examples of genius and their works, you must first empty your soul of the glare of mediocrity, commonness and vulgarity which stamp so much of the world's thought and experience in this day and age. This is why it is good to put yourself into psychic attunement with the classical geniuses whose works have survived the centuries.

14. If you wish to become a great inventor, you can attune your psychic centers to such inventive geniuses as: Eli Whitney, Edison, McCormick, Robert Fulton and Alexander Graham Bell. You can also check up on the lives of other great inventors in history, and use them as psychic mentors to guide you in your own inventions.

How a young man made an inventor of himself

One young man who has studied this system of psychic guidance wanted to become an inventor. He had no special skills but a strong desire to help the world through his ideas. He also wanted to make a fortune so he could endow a scholarship for poor students, who could not afford a technological education. He began to hold conferences with his psychic board of directors, as he called them, consisting of Edison, Fulton and Marconi. He was interested in electronics and automatic electrical equipment, so naturally he went to the source where much of our present-day knowledge of electricity came from— Edison. He would sit in daily psychic sessions and ask his higher psychic centers to contact these great geniuses for ideas that he might perfect in his field.

He would hold imaginary conversations with these experts, and receive their answers, as he expounded his own theories and ideas. Within a period of two years' time this young man, not yet thirty, has perfected twenty-three new ideas for mechanical and electrical inventions and has already placed ten of them with large corporations from whom he will receive royalties for life.

Remember—when you invoke the aid of your psychic imagination in these dialogues with great geniuses, psychic revelations *often come through your imagination!* Someone has rightly called man's imagination "the divine workshop where Cosmic Mind creates all things."

Summary of Chapter 17

1. Your psychic antenna and how to attune it to the wavelength of psychic reception to receive information from geniuses of the past.

2. The psychic reservoir of knowledge, power and fortune which you may tap when you are attuned to high psychic forces.

3. How man may create wings of the soul which can carry him back through time and space to tap the cosmic repository of all creative treasures in the universe.

4. How the soul has a remembrance of past events and how may focus them through your higher psychic centers.

5. How to select the psychic mentor who can guide you, inspire you, and fill your mind with knowledge, inspiration and desire to achieve.

6. The psychic guardian angel who never leaves your side and who can protect you from danger and bring you fulfillment.

7. You can create a psychic whirlpool of inspiration through tapping the minds of the great geniuses of history.

8. The step by step guide for receiving guidance from the geniuses of the past in every department of your life.

9. How to select the special category in which you wish psychic guidance and inspiration.

10. How to hold psychic conferences with Carnegie, Rockefeller and Morgan and be guided to building a financial empire.

11. How to psychically magnetize psychic overtones

from great geniuses and channel their creative power to your daily life.

12. How an inventor, an artist, a lawyer and an author use their psychic attunement to receive guidance in their lives.

chapter 18

How to Create
Security for the Future
Through Psychic Dynamics

We are living in the most advanced and prosperous age in history and yet mankind is afflicted with more wars, problems, poverty and insecurity than he has ever known. On all sides we see political uncertainty, moral degeneration, juvenile delinquency, dope addiction, chronic alcoholism, widespread suicide, and hovering over all—the shadow of the hydrogen bomb threatening mankind with total extinction.

Is it any wonder that you feel at times a deep sense of futility and insecurity?

Do you often long to run to some distant island and escape the maddening confusion of the modern age? Do you feel there is some sanctuary which you can find where you will have peace of mind, inner contentment and feelings of lasting security and permanency?

You are correct in your intuitive feeling that there is a mystical Shangri-la, where you may be secure and contented; a dreamland where everything good can happen to you; a fairy-tale kind of existence where you are surrounded with love, riches, happiness and laughter. But this Shangri-la is only to be discovered through a process of living and thinking, which embraces the philosophy of psychic dynamics.

HOW PSYCHIC DYNAMICS CAN GIVE YOU
NEW VALUES IN LIFE

You can achieve a new understanding of life through the law of *psychic dynamics*. You can be given a complete new and permanent set of values by which to live your life and find the pot of gold at the end of the rainbow, which promises you happiness, peace of mind, love fulfillment and permanency. You can discover the realm of the soul, where the true mystical land of Shangri-la beckons you with its grandeur, dignity, nobility and permanency. When you use these laws of psychic dynamics, you will soar above the mountain peaks of gross materialism, into the mystical realm where dreams are made, and all power, all beauty, all peace, all happiness, all love can be yours.

The meaning of psychic dynamics

What does the term *psychic dynamics* mean?

It relates to the true, dynamic reality which is man's consciousness. It has to do with the mind of man, his soul awareness, his psychic perception; the conscious mind of man is a bridge between two worlds; the world of matter, which we call reality, and the world of psychic reality which we call Cosmic Spirit or Intelligence.

One end of this mystical psychic bridge leads to the physical and material universe, from which we receive stimuli to our senses; the other end leads to the sympathetic nervous system, and the higher mental and spiritual faculties, where we have a high degree of sensitivity to psychic forces. In this realm of the higher mind we receive psychic pulsations, intuitive feelings, automatic guidance; the body cells are all connected with each other, thirty billions of them or more, sending out their silent psychic wavelengths, urging us to eat, to love, to sleep, to repair the body, to heal it when sick, to make money, to reproduce, and, finally to die, leaving the gross physical body behind, while the spiritual side of man, his soul, gloriously traverses the mystic bridge between heaven and earth, to know its ultimate destiny in spiritual freedom, where it may explore the golden realm of spirit.

UNLOCKING THE MYSTIC DOORS OF REALITY THROUGH PSYCHIC DYNAMICS

There is a fourth-dimensional plane of spirit or pure Cosmic Intelligence which exists in the universe. You have the power to unlock the mystic doors of reality through psychic dynamics and live in a world of security and permanency which nothing in this world can mitigate or shatter.

HOW TO USE DESIRE AS A PSYCHIC DYNAMIC KEY

The emotion of desire is inherent in all living things; this includes even the vegetable kingdom, where there may not be conscious desire, but nevertheless, some form of psychic desire exists which makes the seed break out of its prison to become a living, evolving organism.

Science has now discovered that it is *the desire to live* which keeps some people alive, when all medical science says they should have died long ago.

You can release tremendous whirlpools of psychic dynamic energy in your brain and body cells by having this desire to live. More of this life force will flow through your body cells if you *have a reason for living*. It should be, not just to make money, to be comfortable and happy, but to live with a purpose in which you include others in your psychic life plan.

Live for your family.
Live to educate your children.
Live to participate in community activities.
Live to make the world a better place for others.
Live to create, to uplift, to beautify, to educate, to change the world for the better, and you will have tapped inexhaustible reservoirs of psychic dynamic energy to keep you living for a hundred years or more.

HOW TO USE IMAGINATION
AS A PSYCHIC DYNAMIC KEY

We have studied elsewhere in this book about the psychic benefits to be derived from the use of the imagination. Now let us learn how to use imagination as a psychic dynamic key to open mystical doors which can bring you the true beatific vision of greatness and immortality, while you are still on this earth.

It is through the wings of imagination that man may rise into the cosmic realm of spirit, where all his dreams may come true. In the unlimited horizons of minds, man may fly like a bird, and from the womb of time the airplane is born.

In his imagination man may swim like a fish beneath the sea and from this dynamic psychic vision the submarine was created.

The imagination is the psychic connecting link between the Cosmic Mind and man's own consciousness.

HOW TO TRANSFORM YOUR NEGATIVE
ENVIRONMENT WITH PSYCHIC DYNAMICS

When you are imprisoned by a job you hate, use the law of psychic dynamics to transform your environment into something that you can tolerate until you can make a suitable change. Instead of railing against fate and feeling hopelessly trapped, let your imagination build for you a new world, which you will begin to inhabit *now* in the psychic realm, and soon that world of which you dream will become transformed into reality. The future is only a psychic vision of the present; as the past is only a mental reflection that exists nowhere in time and space except in the realm of mind and spirit.

If you are imprisoned by a marriage which has failed to give you emotional security and fulfillment, and you have children, making it impossible to divorce your mate, rise on wings of imagination by using this law of psychic dynamics, and build the romantic world which can transform your prison house into one of kindness, gentility, consideration and beauty. You can work the transforming magic of romance in your present life and discover the unlimited horizons of spiritual and universal love which will make your life glow with hidden beauty.

HOW YOU CAN USE CONCENTRATION AS A PSYCHIC DYNAMIC KEY TO YOUR FUTURE

Psychic dynamics works best when you concentrate the full power of your mind on releasing the higher cosmic energies of your mind, body and soul.

A magnifying glass can be used to concentrate the sun's rays on a piece of paper and set it on fire in a short time.

A ruby is the hardest of all minerals and will not melt in a furnace heated seventy times seven. But if you expose this gem to the concentrated rays of the sun, focused through a glass cube to intensify its rays, *it will disintegrate in a few seconds!*

There is tremendous psychic and cosmic power in concentration. You can use this mystical force to focus the cosmic and psychic rays of the universe in your own mind, and you will be able to dissolve all obstacles, remove all barriers, melt away all resistance and opposition to your goals in the world of matter.

CONCENTRATION STIMULATES THE PSYCHO-NEURAL CENTERS

You can use concentration as a means of stimulating the psycho-neural centers of your brain, where psychic power flows.

Concentrate each day, in psychic meditation, on the dreams you are trying to achieve.

Concentrate in psychic reverie on the flow of creative power from the Cosmic Mind to your brain centers to build the type of world you wish to live in.

See order and harmony where you now live in confusion and discord.

Concentrate on peace and happiness as a psychic reality, where you now are torn with uncertainty and insecurity. See the future as being one of peace and brotherhood, instead of wars, killings and disasters.

Concentrate your psychic power on finding your right place in your work, in your environment at home, and in your social life and love life.

HOW TO USE INSPIRATION AS A PSYCHIC DYNAMIC KEY TO GIVE YOU SECURITY

The word *inspiration* as used here relates to any influence, especially psychic or intuitive, that inspires dynamic thought or action in relation to your life.

We say that an artist is inspired when he creates an artistic work of breathtaking beauty. The inspiration stems from his higher psychic centers and causes him to use psychic dynamics to fashion a great work of art.

Your life is also capable of being an artistic masterpiece when you release the highest form of inspiration in your daily living. It is then that the power of psychic dynamics shapes your life in the perfect images created through your intuitive mind, and you become charged with dynamic energy, life, health and power.

FORCES THAT RELEASE INSPIRATION THROUGH PSYCHIC DYNAMICS

a) Repeat every morning when you awaken, before arising, this inspiring statement to help arouse your psychic centers:

I am created in the image and likeness of God. I am therefore a creative being, capable of releasing tremendous psychic power in my life for creative good.

b) Strive everyday to become inspired by some form of beauty in the outer world. This can be a magnificent painting or a stirring scene from nature. Absorb this pattern of beauty and try to arouse emotions of grandeur and ecstasy, which will help stir your psychic centers with tremendous creative energy.

c) Make it a point to surround yourself with beautiful music in your daily environment, for music stirs the psycho-neural centers of your brain and releases intuitive and psychic action in the nerves of your body, leading to renewed energy and health.

d) The power of good is a well-known force in psychic dynamics. God is good, we are told in the Bible. When you emulate this pattern of cosmic good in your life you become vitally alive and psychically attuned to the highest good in the universe.

e) The emotion of love is one of the most potent forms of releasing psychic dynamics in the brain, body and soul. God is also defined in the Bible as, "God is love." When you are loving and kind, you vibrate to the cosmic pattern of universal love, and a miracle-working power is released in your higher psychic and intuitive centers so that you can literally work miracles of healing the body, overcoming problems, winning friends, and building a destiny of true greatness.

HOW TO USE FAITH AS A KEY OF PSYCHIC DYNAMICS

Faith is one of life's greatest miracle workers. When you want to stir up the power of psychic dynamics in any department of your life, express this positive, life-giving emotion.

Have faith in yourself, knowing that you were created with all the psychic potentials within your consciousness which can guide you to greatness.

Have faith in your future, realizing that without this emotion of confidence in yourself and your future, you lack the psychic dynamics to carry you through the obstacles that threaten every life.

Have faith in other people and believe that they are working for your good. If you think that everyone is out to rob you or hinder and thwart you, the higher psychic centers will be paralyzed and leave you without intuitive guidance.

Have faith in a great Cosmic Intelligence which works through all creation, evolving everything to its highest form of perfection.

If thou canst believe, all things are possible to him that believeth.

It was this power of faith that caused the Miracle-Worker Jesus to perform his amazing psychic miracles of healing and giving new life, and of transmuting matter into new forms.

Summary of Chapter 18

1. Psychic dynamics as a means to combat feelings of insecurity, moral degeneration, and threats to safety.
2. How the philosophy of psychic dynamics reveals the true realm of Shangri-la, where there is peace of mind and security.
3. New values revealed in your life through using the law of psychic dynamics.
4. The mystical psychic bridge that leads to the physical and material universe.
5. The invisible realm where true reality resides and how to discover this permanent realm.
6. The fourth-dimensional plane of spirit where the Cosmic Intelligence exists that rules all creation.
7. The five mystical keys which can be used to channel psychic dynamic power in your everyday life.
8. Desire as a psychic dynamic key to unlock doors to health, happiness and security for the future.

238

9. How to use imagination as a dynamic key to unlock mystical doors to the future.
10. How to transform your negative environment through psychic dynamics.
11. How to use concentration for building psychic power and finding security.
12. How to stimulate the psycho-neural centers of the brain through concentration.
13. The positive forces that release inspiration through psychic dynamics.
14. The power of faith to work miracles in your life and mold your desired future.

chapter 19

How to
Control Matter with
Psycho-Kinematics

You have the power to use your higher psychic mind to change matter and create new forms and substances.

You can project psychic energy through the laws governing psycho-kinematics and turn your ideas into gold.

You can stir the psychic forces in the minds of others and attract them, control them and make them like you.

You can use this power over your own body, changing its chemicals at will, arousing energy, rejuvenating the cells and furnishing drive and motivation for every act of life.

This power to control and change matter is known as Psycho-kinematics, from the two Greek words—kinesis, having to do with action or motion, and psycho, from the word psyche, meaning the mind and soul of man.

In psychic phenomena it has been found by experiments of Dr. J. B. Rhine of Duke University and others in this field, that the human mind could be made to produce a mental and spiritual form of energy that could definitely affect material objects.

In experimenting with dice it was found that some form of mental and electrical energy produced by the human psyche could even control the roll of the dice!

It was further discovered that some form of mental or spiritual energy exists in the universe which can control living plants, move physical objects, break glassware or pottery and in other ways manifest its psychic power and energy.

HOW YOU CAN USE THE POWER OF
PSYCHO-KINEMATICS

You can accept the scientific fact that psycho-kinematics exists as a potent psychic form of energy in the universe. You can tap this field of electro-magnetic energy, which Dr. Rhine called psychokinesis, and affect your own life for positive good.

HOW TO USE THE POWER OF
PSYCHO-KINEMATICS TO CHANGE YOUR LIFE
FOR THE BETTER

1. To project psychic magnetism to your body cells, giving them a stronger life force and energy.

a) Use the key of *desire* to summon the magic genie of your higher psychic mind for stirring the cells with new life force and energy. Desire health, life, energy.

b) Give the psychic command to this higher mind:

I now command the nerves, cells, muscles and organs of my physical body to respond to the higher psychic wavelengths of my mind. I desire health, energy and vitality. I invoke the law of psycho-kinesis, and motivate my body with psychic will.

c) Visualize yourself being strong and healthy. See your body as being eternally young and vital. Radiate energy and vitality from your mind to every part of your body; give the psychic commands.

My heart will now beat in rhythm to the universal and cosmic life force. My stomach works under laws of my higher mind, giving me perfect digestion. My blood circulates in the cosmic pattern of life and health and stimulates my brain and body cells with the cosmic force of eternal life.

d) Now project the inner dream of a perfect body, youth and health to the outer world. Begin to walk in the rhythm of vibrant youth and energy; breathe deeply of the life-giving golden elixir of life, and charge your body cells with dynamic energy. Think young, act young, do the things young people do.

2. How to use the power of psycho-kinematics to heal your body if you should become sick and keep it healthy to an advanced old age.

a) Project to your body cells the mental image of health. If you should be sick, and doctors have diagnosed your illness, try to keep your mind from imprinting this pattern of sickness on your body cells. Realize there is a psychic image of health in the cosmic depository of life, and you will draw upon this psychic image every day of your life to heal you of all negative conditions. Have a desire to live, and live for some specific purpose.

b) Use the mystical keys of visualization and concentration. See with your inner eye, the perfect, healed body operating every day in its usual functions. Stop visualizing sickness as a reality, and remove from your higher psychic centers all fear, worry, hate and anxiety, which produce illness.

c) Project to the outer world the confident, poised, relaxed attitude of perfect health. Do not adopt the pessimistic posture or mental attitude of illness, old age or decrepitude. You can project radiant energy from your higher psychic centers, and they will actually heal your body and keep it healthy.

3. How to project psychic energy to other minds and have them carry out your suggestions and commands.

a) Build the psychic prototype in your mind of the things you want other people to do for you. If you want a raise in salary, hold in the higher mind the face of your boss; talk to him as if you were there in person. The best time to do this is at night, when you have retired and are alone in your room. You can affirm silently, or speak aloud. Use short, simple words and statements such as:

I desire a raise in salary. You know I am worth more money. I give you value for what I receive. You will hear this suggestion that I am projecting to your psychic centers and will respond by giving me that raise.

b) Whenever you see this person, project a golden line of psychic energy to his psychic centers. Bombard his mind with the atomic radiation of your psychic force; see this golden line attached to his brain, and project the words, as with a teletype machine:

I want a raise. Give me more money. Give me the advance to a better job I want. You will recognize my worth. Raise! Money! Money!

c) Emotionalize the psychic force by having a sincere desire for improving your life. See the good that will come through the other person. Visualize yourself doing things that you plan through this psychic projection. Feel the emotions of gratitude, expectation, joy and well-being.

HOW A GIRL PROJECTED THE IMAGE OF LOVE AND MARRIAGE

A very good illustration of how this psychic force works to imprint other minds with the idea you hold, is the story of a girl of twenty-two, who had met a boy in college with whom she fell in love. However, he did not respond to her, until she began to use this method of psycho-kinematics to project her secret dream of love.

She kept this method up for three weeks without any results. Then one day her phone rang and a boy named Bob asked her to go to a football game. She went, and there, with another girl, was the boy she had been in love with for two years!

She had projected the desire of love and marriage to this boy, whose name was Ted. When she saw him this time, she projected the thought with the psycho-kinematic suggestions: *I still love you. Why don't you love me? You will call me up for a date. I want to marry you.* She kept up this type of psychic bombardment of his psychic centers, and suddenly Ted was standing beside her, without his girl, asking her for a date! She gave him her number and told him to call her. The next day he was on the phone, and after their first date, he told her he never realized he was in love with her until he saw her with another boy! He did not know that his psychic centers were aroused with the emotional projection she had made. Of course they were married, and there is every chance that they will be happy forever after!

This girl used our three mystical keys to summon the psychic magic genie of her higher mind to help her; the key of *desire;* the key of *visualization,* and the key of *projection.*

4. How to use psycho-kinematics to materialize money, houses, lands, stocks, automobiles and other riches.

a) Build desire in your psychic centers by wanting the money or other objects that you wish. Have a clear-cut idea of what you want to do with the money, or how you intend to use the objects you are asking for.

How a maid and butler attracted a fortune

A man and his wife came to my lectures in Carnegie Hall some years ago. They came to see me for a personal interview and told me of their dream; they wanted to be rich and successful, but they worked as maid and butler for a rich widower in New Jersey. I told them of this method for using psycho-kinematics to attract money. I remember the man said, "But Mr. Norvell, we do not make a big salary—how can we ever make enough money to invest and build a fortune?"

Then this man told me of a dream he and his wife had; to create a home for talented children who showed signs of being artistic but who were too poor to afford building careers in the arts. They started using the method given here for attracting money and property, and came to the lectures frequently over a period of five years.

One day I picked up the *New York Times* and read a story that amazed me. A rich man had died and left his entire estate worth over half a million dollars, including an enormous home and swimming pool to his faithful maid and butler who had worked for him over a period of twenty years! It was the maid and butler who had been projecting the dream through psycho-kinematics that they would one day be rich and able to help children!

b) In psychic reverie, practice holding in the forefront of your consciousness the picture of the thing you are trying to materialize. If it is money, see the things that the money will buy; if you are asking for ten thousand dollars, visualize it in terms of a payment on a home you wish to buy; a car, a fur coat, a portfolio of stocks, a piano, a trip around the world—whatever you wish to do with the money. This will create a psychic facsimile of money and stir your psychic centers into dynamic action.

How a woman projected a trip to Europe free

One member of my lecture group in New York wanted a trip to London, but she had no large sum of money with which to take this trip. She began to project to a Cosmic Mind someone who was planning to go to Europe, and also the picture of her accompanying this unknown person. *She knew of no such wealthy person,* but one day, after she had projected this picture about two weeks, her phone rang. A voice said, "You do not know me, but a friend of mine told me that you might be free to accompany me on a trip to Europe as a companion." It turned out that this elderly lady needed someone to help her on such a trip and she was psychically guided to this woman. She went on the trip, not only to London, but to Paris, Rome and Amsterdam, and it cost her nothing!

c) Begin to visualize yourself having the things you want in life. Remember, matter can be affected by the power of your mind and soul. There is a substance known as spiritual protoplasm in the invisible universe, it is constanly being molded and shaped by creative mind power. You can exert this power through psycho-kinematics.

d) Write down a list of the things you want to magnetize or attract. Read this list over every morning and night, and concentrate the power of your higher psychic mind on projecting the thought forms and pictures to the invisible Cosmic Mind. Use photographs, pictures and illustrations from newspapers and magazines to make these pictures more real.

5. How to use psycho-kinematics to project magnetism to others and attract them in business or other departments of your life.

a) You can bombard your psychic centers with magnetic thoughts and arouse so much emotional energy that others will feel your presence. Have you not seen people enter a room who were so magnetic that every head turned to look at them? You are able to project this type of psychic magnetism by having a desire to be a powerful and magnetic personality.

b) Fill your consciousness with magnetic thoughts; goodness, charity, love, beauty, peace, happiness and optimism; these are psychic and magnetic currents that arouse the minds of others. When you meet a person send out a radiant stream of psychic energy. Mentally say to yourself, "I like you and you are going to like me. I want to be your friend. I want to be in business with you. I can help you and you will help me." Keep your thoughts simple and uninvolved, being certain that you are sincere, that you feel emotion, and that you are only projecting what will be for the other person's good, as well as your own.

How this power worked in a social situation

Mrs. R. lived in a new community where she had not yet been fully accepted into the social life. Her husband was an attorney and it was important that they win acceptance. Mrs. R. had studied psychic laws and knew about psycho-kinematics. There was one social hostess, the wife of a big judge in their city, who was the social pivot around which the community revolved. Mrs. R. had met this woman at a local meeting of the PTA. But the woman had shown no unusual interest in her.

One day Mrs. R. heard that this woman, Mrs. W., was giving a party at her home the next week. She had not been invited. Mrs. R. began to work to project a stream of psychic energy; she enlisted the aid of her psychic magic genie, and each day she sent out this positive command: "Mrs. W., you will send my husband and me an invitation to your party. I need your help and will be grateful to you for this invitation. I shall do everything I can to be a credit to the community." She kept up this type of psychic bombardment of Mrs. W.'s psychic centers. On a Friday, the day before the party, Mrs. R.'s phone rang; it was Mrs. W. She said, "I remember meeting you at the PTA meeting, and my husband and I would like to have you both come to a party we're giving tomorrow night for a group of friends. I'm sorry to have waited this long to invite you."

Mrs. R. and her husband went to this woman's home, and they were introduced to the judge, who later turned out to be a valuable contact in Mr. R.'s legal work. Undoubtedly Mrs. W. felt the stirring of psychic energy through the power of psycho-kinematics that was projected from Mrs. R.'s mind.

6. How you can use psycho-kinematics to inspire every person who comes into your environment with the magic circle of charm, beauty and magnetism.

a) People respond to the subtle vibrations that issue from your higher mind. When you project the stirring psychic energy of your secret thoughts, people respond without knowing why. When you meet people, mentally surround them with an aura of beauty and charm. You can crystallize this by thinking of the aura you are projecting as being golden and radiant. I call this the magic circle. You project this golden circle of psychic energy like a pair of loving arms, surrounding and enfolding the person you wish to enchant with its invisible magic.

b) At the same time that you project this magic circle to enfold the other person, psychically send them the telepathic communication:

I now enfold you in the magic circle of beauty and enchantment. You will feel my golden aura of love. You will respond with friendliness, happiness and kindness.

How a great singer uses this secret to hold her audiences

I remember once at Carnegie Hall a famous singer was backstage, and I talked with her before one of her sold-out concerts. I asked her the secret of her great power and beautiful voice. She remarked, "When I am on the stage singing to an audience, I feel that my voice is like a pair of loving arms, embracing the entire audience, reaching way up into the farthest reaches of the balcony, encircling every member of that audience, and I love every person out there."

This was the cause of her greatness; she was using the laws of psycho-kinematics instinctively to win and hold her audiences, and her voice reflects the vibrancy, beauty and enchantment that goes with such a spiritually evolved person.

c) Practice using this secret power of psychic magnetism, by projecting your thought forms to people in the same room with you at a party. Visualize them being tied to you by lines of radiant psychic energy that are pure gold. Vibrate those lines of energy by holding interesting thoughts in mind. Project the thought form of friendship, value, beauty, good and happiness. The psychic flow of energy will illuminate your face with an inner glow that will make you irresistible.

8. How to use psycho-kinematics to produce inspiration for creative work, bodily health and long life.

a) The psychic energy that you radiate from the higher centers of your brain is produced by your emotions. Instill various emotions when you wish to stir up a whirlpool of psychic energy for creative work. The emotion of desire will form thought waves of intense power.

b) Have a desire for fame and fortune, and the psychic forces within you will guide you to paths where you may achieve fame and fortune.

c) Have a desire to create beauty in all forms. This furnishes your creative centers with the inspiration to produce works of art, literature, music and design.

d) Visualize yourself becoming famous as a result of

248

your creative ideas. Emulate the great thoughts of artists, musicians, composers, authors, designers, and other creative geniuses by studying their lives. Psycho-kinematics works best when you stir the higher creative and psychic centers into vibrant action. This can be done by duplicating the thought processes of geniuses, as we have learned elsewhere in this study.

9. How to use psycho-kinematics to transform ideas into riches and live a life of glamor and beauty.

a) There is a great cosmic law known as *transmutation,* which you may use to change matter through the power of psycho-kinematics. Science now can change living, growing things by bombarding the invisible genes with ultra-violet rays and other substances that produce mutations, new breeds, amazing fruits, flowers and vegetables, giant-sized chickens and other animals. You can use the radiatory power of your mind to transmute matter, to change it from one form to another; to create new products, inventions, chemicals, scientific discoveries which can help the world. Your mind can be the cyclotron which bombards your ideas with the radioactive substance of spirit.

b) Hold in your higher mind the thought that you wish to transform into substance and gold. Perhaps it is an idea for a new business, an invention, a dramatic story, or a song that can make you a fortune. Visualize that creative idea being given to the world and being accepted. Sit daily in psychic reverie and ask for guidance in bringing your idea into the world, and the guidance will come.

One man projected the psychic image of a little button-hole, and that idea was transmuted from his psychic centers into a million dollar fortune.

Another man thought of a collar button, and the stream of gold began pouring in.

Still other men thought of the typewriter, the air-conditioner, the vacuum cleaner, the washing machine, and the thousands of other household appliances; and the psychic centers were stirred with the power to create the thing which they had mentally imaged.

c) Psycho-kinematic power exists in creative thoughts. Form your thoughts into creative patterns, and visualize the finished product being used by millions. Or you may have an inspiration to go into a business where you will make a fortune.

One man stirred this type of psychic energy into action some years ago. He had a little push cart on the street, from which he sold his ice cream. Finally his psycho-kinematic power projected to someone who offered him a fortune for his formula and one of the world's greatest chains of restaurants was born. This man retired with millions.

d) Instead of sitting back and envying the rich and glamorous, set to work to transform your own life into patterns of beauty, glamor and happiness. Stir psychic energy in your higher centers by a process of accultura-tion of your mind. Study great thoughts of other minds; cmulate patterns of conduct and action which others who are successful have used. Associate with people who will inspire you and uplift you. Go to evening school and study public speaking, so you can better express your creative ideas.

Summary of Chapter 19

1. How your mind can shape and mold matter through the law of psycho-kinematics.
2. How to use the power of psycho-kinematics to project magnetism and life to your body cells for health and long life.
3. How to project creative energy to materialize money and other objects through psycho-kine-matics.
4. How you can use this power to attract people in business and romance and shape the thinking of others.
5. How to stir the psycho-neural centers of your brain and release psychic energy to color your environment and personality.
6. The three mystical keys that can be used to summon up the power of your higher mind.

250

7. Step by step method to use psycho-kinematics to change your entire life for the better.

8. How you can have better health by projecting the inner dream of a perfect body to your higher psychic centers.

9. How to give psychic commands and suggestions to other people and have them carry out your every wish for good.

10. A golden line of psychic energy to bombard the psychic centers of people that you wish to influence to receive advance in salary or position, or to change your life.

11. The method for materializing money, houses, lands, stocks and bonds, and other treasures that you desire in your life.

12. How one woman projected a free trip to Europe through the power of psycho-kinematics.

13. One woman used this power of psycho-kinematics to change a social situation and win acceptance in a high social circle.

14. How a singer's great voice was aided by the secret power of psycho-kinematics.

15. How you can use psycho-kinematics to transform ideas and thoughts into a radiant stream of gold and power that will bless your life with riches and abundance.

chapter 20

The Techniques of Psychic Programming to Get What You Want in Life

A whole new world of power awaits your joyous discovery when you once learn how to use the secret of *psychic programming* to create anything you want in life.

Just as man can now press a button and send a rocket weighing thousands of pounds into space, so too, you can set off a powerful chain reaction of psychic and atomic energy in your consciousness and release miraculous forces which can propel you to a great destiny by using this secret technique of psychic programming.

With this method of psychic chain reaction, you can feed into the higher, automatic centers of your mind the commands, desires, ambitions, dreams and aspirations you want to achieve, and then the psychic mechanism of your mind will automatically set to work to create the conditions that you have programmed into your consciousness.

The modern electronic computer has added a new word to our language: *programming*. This relates to the ability of a computer to receive into its elaborate electronic network certain statistical facts and data, which it puts through its computer brain. When certain information is desired the computer can, in a few moments' time, bring forth amazingly involved calculations, information and answers to problems that might take a dozen men weeks to compute.

We can utilize this same principle in what I call psychic programming. You can use the higher psychic centers of your brain exactly like an electronic computer for mental telepathy, clairvoyance and intuition. These higher psychic centers work through principles of magnetism and electricity. They work independently of your conscious mind, which has the ability to choose events consciously, to rationalize, and to exercise will power, but which does not have the higher psychic visions which exist in the computer-like regions of the higher psychic mind.

THE THREE MINDS WHICH MAN MAY USE

There are three minds which man may use for guidance in his life. Each has its specific function and may be tapped for various purposes.

1. The *conscious* mind, which gives us awareness through our five senses of the outer and inner world.

2. The *subconscious* mind, which is the automatic brain that causes us to breathe and which makes the heart beat, the blood circulate, the stomach digest and the body heal.

3. The *superconscious* mind, which is the supersensible realm where intuition, psychic phenomena, clairvoyance and other extrasensory powers reside.

How to use your conscious mind in psychic programming

1. Choose the events that you want your higher psychic mind to externalize in your life, your body, your environment, and the situations that you will attract.

2. Make out a psychic computer program, in which you list on paper all the things that you desire. Your chart might look like this.

a) The type of work I want to do in the future.
b) The social life I desire.
c) The type of friends I want to make.
d) The gifts and talents I would like to have.
e) The knowledge and cultural benefits that I expect.
f) The romance and marriage I want in the future.
g) The type of home I want to live in.
h) The size family I want to have.
i) The income I would like for security.
j) The investments I would like to make.
k) The mental and bodily health I desire.
l) The personality I wish to develop.

m) The problems I want to overcome.

n) The negative habits that I wish to conquer.

You might add extra items such as specific sums of money you would like for certain purposes.

You might want to attract a certain important person who can help you in your business affairs.

You might want to remove an unwanted situation in your life or environment that keeps you from being happy.

You might want to take a trip to some part of the world, and may not have the means to do so.

Any of these desires can be fed consciously into your psychic computer, through this process of psychic programming, and you will receive guidance for achieving the fulfillment of that which you desire.

How to use your subconscious mind in psychic programming

Your subconscious mind is the intermediary between the psychic receptors of your superconscious mind and your conscious mind centers.

You can psychically program into this subconscious mind any of the elements given above, if you will observe these rules for your guidance.

1. Repeat the instructions several times consciously, either by writing them out, or saying them aloud so your subconscious mind will absorb the instructions.

2. Make it a habit to give this subconscious mind the psychic programming each day as a regular habit. The best time to choose for this type of subconscious suggestion is at night, just before you retire.

3. Repeat each psychic suggestion over at least ten times. You can use as many as you wish, but do not overburden the psychic mechanism by making too many suggestions at one time. Spread them out over a period of weeks or months, gradually feeding these suggestions into the sensitized computer of the psychic centers of your superconscious mind.

4. Write out a list of the things you wish to program

psychically so as to imprint them upon your subconscious mind more forcibly. You can make this list out in your own handwriting, then keep it on a wall in your room where you see it often. Read this list over every morning upon arising, and every night before retiring. These items that you psychically program through your subconscious will be working into your superconscious mind all day and all night, and suddenly, out of the blue, you will be given the psychic guidance for achieving whatever it is that you have programmed in your psychic centers.

*How to use your superconscious mind in
psychic programming*

It is through your superconscious mind that you can tap the automatic psychic realm where you receive intuitive guidance, mental telepathy and clairvoyant vision for directing your life in the future.

It is possible to tap this superconscious realm through this regime:

1. Sit in psychic reverie and let your mind concentrate on receiving psychic messages from the atmosphere. You can hold another person's face in your consciousness, and ask information about that person, or you can let thoughts come into your mind from other channels.

2. You can project your mind to distant places and ask for clairvoyant visions of things you wish information about.

3. You can appeal to this superconscious mind for special knowledge and information on any subject you choose.

4. You can ask questions about how to solve your problems, whom you should trust, if you should go into business with a certain person; if you should marry a certain man or woman.

5. You can instruct this superconscious mind as to the gifts and talents you wish to develop and it will reveal how to go about painting, writing, composing music, inventing, or anything else you choose.

HOW TO USE PSYCHIC STIMULATORS FOR LIFE-PROGRAMMING

To release potent psychic power within your super-conscious mind, you can feed into the computer of your higher mind the ideas, thought forms and words which will help stimulate these centers and release a stream of new combinations of ideas—original concepts, brilliant thoughts —that will help you achieve your goals in life.

The following twenty-five psychic stimulators may be memorized or written down and consulted so you can psychically program them into your higher mind centers. These thoughts will set up psychic chain reactions, communicating to all your brain centers, and releasing new and original combinations of ideas. Then, like a computer, your psychic centers will release these stimulating thoughts into new life patterns of positive and constructive action. You will be automatically driven in the direction of goal achievement through this technique of psychic programming.

The following twenty-five psychic stimulators have been selected from some of the greatest geniuses of the past—but you can use others, or make up your own—and they may fit any category or subject upon which you wish psychic guidance and direction.

After you have read over the twenty-five psychic stimulators, read carefully the instructions that follow for using them in relation to any of the goals that you desire in your future life.

USE THESE TWENTY-FIVE PSYCHIC STIMULATORS FROM GREAT MINDS TO SET UP CHAIN REACTIONS IN THE COMPUTER OF YOUR HIGHER MIND

• HONESTY

> I hope I shall always possess firmness and virtue enough to maintain

what I consider the most desirable of all titles, the character of an honest man.

Washington

• TRUTHFULNESS

This above all: to thine own self be true, And it must follow, as the night the day, Thou canst not then be false to any man.

Shakespeare

• CHARACTER

Character is a diamond that scratches every other stone.

Bertol

• PATIENCE

He that can have patience, can have what he will.

Franklin

• PEACE

Five enemies to peace inhabit with us: avarice, ambition, envy, anger and pride. If these enemies were to be banished, we should infallibly enjoy perpetual peace.

Petrarch

• HOPE

A propensity to hope and joy is real riches; one to fear and sorrow, real poverty.

Hume

• IDEALS

The best and noblest lives are those which are set toward high ideals.

Almeron

• IMAGINATION

Imagination rules the world.

Napoleon

• TOLERANCE

It is not a merit to tolerate, but rather a crime to be intolerant.

Shelley

- SUCCESS

If you wish success in life, make perseverance your bosom friend, experience your wise counselor, caution your elder brother, and hope your guardian genius.

Addison

- CONSIDERATION

Consideration is the soil in which wisdom may be expected to grow, and strength be given to every up-springing plant of duty.

Emerson

- PATRIOTISM

After what I owe to God, nothing should be more dear or more sacred than the love and respect I owe to my country.

De Thou

- SELF-CONTROL

No man is free who cannot command himself.

Pythagoras

- COURAGE

Courage is, on all hands, considered as an essential of high character.

Froude

- GENEROSITY

True generosity is a duty as indispensably necessary as those imposed on us by law. It is a rule imposed by reason, which should be the sovereign law of a rational being.

Goldsmith

- HONOR

Life every man holds dear; but the dear man holds honor far more precious dear than life.

Shakespeare

• FREEDOM

Freedom of religion, freedom of the press, and freedom of person under the protection of the habeas corpus, these are principles that have guided our steps through an age of revolution and reformation.

Jefferson

• KNOWLEDGE

I had six honest serving men,
They taught me all I knew:
Their names were Where and What and When,
And Why and How and Who.

Rudyard Kipling

• LOVE

We are shaped and fashioned by what we love.

Goethe

• HAPPINESS

No man is happy who does not think himself so.

Marcus Aurelius Antoninus

• FORGIVENESS

To err is human; to forgive, divine.

Pope

• INDUSTRIOUSNESS

If you have great talents, industry will improve them; if moderate abilities, industry will supply their deficiencies. Nothing is denied to well-directed labor; nothing is ever to be attained without it.

Sir Joshua Reynolds

• RESPONSIBILITY

Responsibility walks hand in hand with capacity and power.

J. G. Holland

- SELF-CONFIDENCE

> Doubt whom you will, but never doubt yourself.
>
> Bouvee

- FAITH

> Faith marches at the head of the army of progress. It is found beside the most refined life, the freest government, the profoundest philosophy, the noblest poetry, the purest humanity.
>
> T. T. Munger

HOW TO FEED PSYCHIC STIMULATORS INTO YOUR SUPERCONSCIOUS MIND

Let us now study the method for ·using psychic programming for specific things you desire in your life.

Let us assume you are asking for psychic guidance for Category *(a)*—The type of work' I want to do in the future.

As you sit in psychic reverie, feed into the psychic computer system of your superconscious and conscious minds the following psychic stimulators (keyed from the master list of twenty-five psychic stimulators from great minds).

Key
3. *Character*
4. *Patience*
6. *Hope*
8. *Imagination*
10. *Success*
18. *Knowledge*
22. *Industriousness*

Repeat the psychic stimulators from great minds found under the headings of *Character, Patience, Hope, Imagination, Success, Knowledge, Industriousness*. These key words will set up a chain reaction with related psychic thoughts hidden in your higher brain centers, and trigger a complete psychic set-up of new ideas, inspiration and intuitive guidance which will help you direct your life energies to the work you should do in the future.

Then let us say that you want to psychically program in your superconscious mind the idea embodied in Item (f)—The romance and marriage I want in the future.

You will feed into the psychic computer of your higher mind the following psychic stimulators, repeating the sentences under each heading, absorbing their meaning and letting your mind respond to the psychic chain reactions that they will set into motion.

Key
7. *Ideals*
9. *Tolerance*
11. *Consideration*
13. *Self-control*
15. *Generosity*
16. *Honor*
19. *Love*
20. *Happiness*
21. *Forgiveness*
23. *Responsibility*
25. *Faith*

The sentences embodying the above words in your higher psychic centers, will set up reactions that will propel you to think, feel and do the things implied by the above psychic stimulators.

You can write the various psychic stimulators on little cards which you carry in your purse or wallet and look at several times a day, until the quotations are a part of your mental and psychic mechanism. Your mind will be conditioned in the pattern of thought that is symbolized by the words and sentences you have repeated.

If you wish to psychically program Item (1)—The personality I wish to develop, you would study, repeat, and memorize the sentences found under the following key psychic stimulators:

Key
1. *Honesty*
2. *Truthfulness*
3. *Character*
4. *Patience*
5. *Peace*
6. *Hope*
7. *Ideals*
9. *Tolerance*
11. *Consideration*
13. *Self-control*
14. *Courage*
15. *Generosity*
16. *Honor*
24. *Self-confidence*

You could also add *Love, Faith,* and *Forgiveness* to the sentences you psychically program, for they would all add to the sum total of chain reactions you would set up in wishing to develop a strong, dynamic and forceful personality.

You can use Biblical quotations or make up your own psychic stimulators. Two very good ones to use for all purposes are the twenty-third and the ninety-first Psalm.

These psychic pictures may be of the car you want to own, the home you wish to buy and live in; the furniture you desire; the clothing, jewelry, refrigerator, air-conditioner, television set, boat, or any other object that you want to materialize.

Examples of successful psychic programming

Feed these psychic pictures to your mental computer at least once a day and keep it up until you attract them.

I have known people who have used this system of psychic stimulation and who have received sums of money from ten thousand to a quarter of a million dollars; others have concentrated on homes they wanted and they were guided to find and finance those homes. One lady fed her picture of a five thousand dollar mink coat into her psychic computer, and she received it as a gift from a wealthy woman who bought a new one. There was no verbal communication between them prior to this action. The psychic computer triggered the higher centers of the donor's mind and she voluntarily gave the other woman the fur coat!

A lecture member psychically programmed an expensive hi-fi set with speakers for his home. He didn't have the available cash to buy one at the time. Within two weeks a friend, leaving for Europe, *gave him the exact equipment he had programmed!*

HOW TO USE PSYCHIC SENSORS IN YOUR PROGRAMMING OF FUTURE EVENTS

Psychic sensors work through your higher mind to cause you to avoid certain actions that might be detrimental to your future health, welfare or existence.

These psychic sensors are programmed or conditioned in your automatic reflexes of the sympathetic nervous system through training, education, social mores, and religious training.

When you go to steal someone else's property, some psychic sensor says: "Don't steal that; you will be caught and imprisoned." Or the psychic computer rings the alarm bell: *Thou shalt not steal!*

If you go to injure or kill another person, the psychic computer, if it has been correctly programmed, screams, "Don't commit acts of violence for you will be punished!" Or the psychic computer will bring from your psychic centers the admonition: *Thou shalt not kill!*

If you over-drink, over-eat, or over-smoke, this psychic sensor releases from the computer of your superconscious: "Stop! You are endangering your health by this action! Use moderation in all things." If you listen to this psychic sensor, you will live longer, be healthier and survive in the future.

THE TEN POSITIVE FORCES TO FEED YOUR PSYCHIC COMPUTER TO OVERCOME NEGATIVE FORCES

Sit in psychic silence for at least an hour a day, while you are treating the ten negative forces that you wish to overcome. You will feed into your psychic computer the ten positive forces given here to inhibit and overcome all those negative habits that might pose a threat against your future health, happiness, prosperity, peace and security.

Repeat each of the following psychic inhibitors at least five times. Write them down on filing cards and each day take a new one in your purse, and all day, whenever you see this card, repeat that particular psychic inhibitor. Soon those positive inhibitors will become so much a part of your psychic programming system that they will automatically be projected into the forefront of your consciousness when you are confronted with any negative situation in your life.

1. I now instruct my superconscious mind to feed into the psychic computer that regulates my habits and daily actions this positive programming: I shall overcome all tendencies to negative habits that threaten mental and physical well-being. I wish to express strength of will power to triumph over all personal weaknesses, such as indolence, procrastination, disorder, smoking, drinking, gambling, or any other habits that are detrimental to my future. I desire in my future psychic programming of those habits only which are positive and helpful.

2. I now psychically program a positive regime which will help me overcome bad temper, anger, and a tendency to be quarrelsome with other people in my work and my home. I ask psychic guidance for mental and emotional control. I have a desire to live at peace with others and now ask my higher psychic centers to guide me to maintain calmness in the face of disorder, to exercise patience when confronted with hostility, and to say the right things when others' behavior tends to anger me.

3. I wish to overcome all tendencies to moodiness, fits of depression and despondency. I realize that these negative forces can destroy my peace and mental equilibrium. I now feed into the psychic computer of my mind the positive forces of optimism, hope, faith, expectation and radiant acquiescence. I accept life in all its many manifestations, and react only with joy and enthusiasm.

4. I imprint upon my higher psychic centers now the desire to operate on a level of honesty, truth and moral integrity in every situation that confronts me. I wish to dispel the negative forces of dishonesty, lying, cheating and stealing. I now psychically program moral, ethical, social and spiritual conduct that obeys the Ten Commandments, and the high psychic principles of the Golden Rule and the Sermon on the Mount.

5. I now project to my mental and psychic centers the positive principle that all things come to him who waits. I wish to psychically program into my higher mind centers the qualities of patience, tolerance and reasonableness. I am aware that I have a rendezvous with destiny and there is no haste. All good will come to me, if I practice patience and tolerance.

6. I wish to invoke the law of psychic inhibitors to overcome the forces of egotism, boastfulness and sefishness. I wish to psychically program the fact that the *I am,* higher self is always in control and my qualities of integrity, honor and worth will express themselves perfectly in my outer and inner life. I adopt the attitude of selflessness, knowing that when I give to the world, my good will always be returned.

7. I now involve in my psychic computer the emotion of love, knowing that it will negate the forces of hatred, bigotry and intolerance. I wish to express love for my fellow-men, for my country and for the Cosmic Godhead which created all things.

8. I am now abundantly blessed and recognize the universal law of justice and generosity. My psychic forces shall be motivated to give fair measure to everyone I meet, to express charity, forgiveness and compassion when others are in need.

9. My psychic centers are now programmed for con-

fidence, peace and poise to combat the negative forces of fear, worry and anxiety which erode the mind and soul. I wish to master fear in all its phases and its related emotions of envy, greed, intolerance, jealousy and hate.

10. I recognize that hostlity towards others is hostility towards myself. I now exercise the psychic inhibitor of understanding of others' weaknesses, and adopt a pacifist's attitude towards the world and other people. I pour the balm of peace upon the troubled waters of my environment and I express only outward calm and tranquility.

Summary of Chapter 20

1. How to use the psychic programming for stirring the higher centers of consciousness to produce telepathy, clairvoyance, and intuition for the benefits they alone can bestow.

2. The three minds which you possess and how to use each to receive psychic guidance in your life.

3. Psychic programming to feed into your higher centers the work you want, the money you wish to attract, the social and romantic life you desire.

4. The part the subconscious mind plays in psychic programming, for establishing automatic mental telepathy and clairvoyance.

5. The power of your superconscious mind and how to tap this power through psychic programming.

6. How to use psychic stimulators to stir the superconscious mind.

7. The twenty-five psychic stimulators that will produce the most powerful dynamic action in the higher psychic mind.

8. How people have used psychic programming to get free a mink coat and an expensive hi-fi set.

9. The ten positive forces to overcome any negative habits and free you to live in health, happiness, prosperity and tranquility.

FIRST TIME IN PAPERBACK!

HELPING YOURSELF WITH
SELF-HYPNOSIS

By Frank S. Caprio, M.D.
and Joseph R. Berger

Self-hypnosis may be the means of solving all your problems. This amazing, successfully tested book shows you how to:

- Put yourself under a hypnotic trance—yet keep total awareness and control

- Give yourself commands to change and improve your life—to stop smoking—to lose weight—improve your memory

- Rouse yourself from the hypnotic state with perfect ease and safety

- Achieve the goals you set for yourself in your self-induced hypnotic state

Try this simple, programmed technique of self-hypnosis and get more of what you want out of life!

64-022, 75¢